THE **NEW WORLD** OF
RETIREMENT
A GUIDE BOOK

DAVID HERSTLE JONES III

This document discusses general concepts for retirement planning, and is not intended to provide tax or legal advice. Individuals are urged to consult with their tax and legal professionals regarding these issues. This handbook should ensure that clients understand a) that annuities and some of their features have costs associated with them; b) that income received from annuities is taxable; and c) that annuities used to fund IRAs do not afford any additional measure of tax deferral for the IRA owner.

Printed in the United States of America

First Printing, 2014

Gradient Positioning Systems, LLC
4105 Lexington Avenue North, Suite 110
Arden Hills, MN 55126 (877) 901-0894

Contributors: Nick Stovall, Nate Lucius, Mike Binger and Gradient Positioning Systems, LLC.

ACKNOWLEDGEMENTS

First, I would like to thank my wife, Kelly, for always being my biggest supporter, and my two beautiful children, Holden and Kiana, who are the inspiration for all of my hard work. Thank you to my entire staff, the daily display of all of your dedication never goes unnoticed. Lastly, I would like to thank Nick Stovall, Nate Lucius, Mike Binger, Wayne Schmidt and the rest of my associates for their contributions. Team work truly does make the dream work.

TABLE OF CONTENTS

INTRODUCTION

Welcome to the new world.

No matter who you are or how robust your retirement savings might be, one thing is for sure: you've noticed that today's world is different.

Most of us can remember a time when people invested money in the stock market, left it where it was for thirty years, and retired comfortably. Perhaps you had grandparents with pensions who invested every penny of their savings in bank CDs and earned a healthy return that paid for your college.

By now, you already know that things have changed.

The market is different. Even if you haven't spent time analyzing and studying the stock market, you likely know someone (or ten people, or twenty) whose retirement savings got hit hard in the 2001 economic downturn or who lost big in the bear market that began in 2008. Even without hard numbers, you probably already know that the market has become more volatile in the last couple of decades. But, just in case, we've got some hard numbers for you anyway.

The S&P 500 (Standard & Poors) is one of the broadest and most diverse barometers of the U.S. financial market, and, as a result, its numbers offer a clear picture of the market's overall performance over time. Consider this chart, which shows how the market has performed over the last 40 years:

This chart created by author using historical price data of the S&P 500 as reported by Yahoo! Finance.

See that? You've probably heard of bear markets and bull markets, but there's another way to look at it. From the mid-1970s to the mid-1990s, we had a **tortoise market**: slow, steady, and always winning. Since the mid-1990s, however, we've switched to a **hare market**: Big, abrupt gains with equally massive and sudden losses. Why the switch? A lot of factors have contributed to our new market of extremes. For one, in the Internet age, information travels fast and impacts the market almost as quickly. In the new world, political upheaval on the other side of the planet can have adverse effects on the American financial market almost immediately. Add to that the fact that millions of individual traders can make instant changes to their portfolios, and you've got a real roller coaster ride. After all, volatility often leads to more volatility.

For example, on Wednesday, August 10, 2011, the Dow Jones Industrial Average, another respected measure of the market's performance, plunged 520 points, which represents its ninth-worst point loss ever. Just one day before, however, the Dow rose a breathtaking 430 points.* That's just a snapshot of a period marked by extraordinary peaks and valleys. As we'll discuss in Chapter 7, this kind of volatility causes individual investors to react emotionally. Take Douglas, for example.

Douglas came to visit us in Aug. 2011. He was 60, and three years earlier, in 2008, he had lost 30 percent of his retirement savings. He was 57 then, so Douglas, who was managing his own stock portfolio online, decided that the only option was to increase his stock holdings, hoping to make up the difference. But the volatility continued. By 2011, Douglas was sick with worry. The market was up and down nearly every day, and by the time Douglas came to see us, he was pale with anxiety.

---

*http://money.cnn.com/2011/08/10/markets/markets_newyork/

"I want out," Douglas said immediately. He was sitting in our conference room, his hands clenched in front of him. "If I lose any more of my savings, I won't be able to retire at all. Let's just put it in a CD and be done."

Unfortunately, that wasn't a good solution either, since a bank CD wouldn't even keep Douglas ahead of inflation. But fortunately, we DID have some good solutions. We helped Douglas create an income plan that allowed him to earn enough return to beat the risks, such as inflation, but still keep his money safe. He retired on time, thanks to the fact that he followed his instincts and sought out a professional financial team.

Douglas reacted emotionally to his portfolio losses, and who wouldn't? This is your savings on the line, your quality of life. That's why it's important to have an objective financial professional on your team—to prevent you from making emotional decisions about your finances. First Douglas went all in, like a gambler at a craps table who just lost half his money, hoping to beat the house. Then, when he realized nobody beats the house, he wanted to take all his money out and put it in the bank. But traditional forms of income strategies—old world strategies—like CDs, bonds and treasury notes, simply don't work anymore for primary income strategies. Thanks to rising inflation and historically low interest rates, they don't earn enough yield to keep retirees ahead of inflation, and that means a real and terrifying risk of running out of money.

Bank Certificates of Deposit (CDs) were once a safe way to grow your money for future income. According to the Federal Reserve Economic Data database, CDs had a healthy 5.20 percent rate of return even as recently as in the year 2000. Currently, however, the database shows that CDs are only delivering a yield of less than one percent, which is well below the average inflation rate of 3 percent. That means your investment would be losing more than 2 percent of its buying power every year.

U.S. Treasury Notes have also long been considered a safe way to grow your savings and generate a comfortable income. According to the Board of Governors of the Federal Reserve System, 10-year Treasury Notes had an annual maturity rate of 6.75 percent in the year 2000. This means that if you bought a 10-year Treasury Note valued at $100,000 in the year 2000, then you could count on $6,750 in annual income from that investment. Today, 10-year Treasury Notes have an annual maturity rate of 2.95 percent. Consequently, that same 10-year Treasury Note for $100,000 would give you less than half of that income: $2,950 per year. This is not too comfortable.

So where does that leave us? The stock market is a roller coaster, making it nearly impossible, and certainly very painful, to manage our own portfolios successfully. Traditional safe ways to grow your savings and generate income are either no longer effective or no longer safe—or both. What's a soon-to-be-retired person to do? *Find the right Advisory team.*

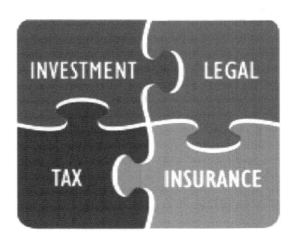

In the new world of retirement, you need an advisory team that can offer you efficient, innovative solutions for your retirement plan. So what should you look for in a retirement planning team? In order to create a comprehensive and efficient retirement solution, you need experts working together from all of the BIG FOUR areas:

Imagine the sound of a violin. It's beautiful, right? Well, it's beautiful when it's played well. I won't play violin for you. You'd be much happier with me as your Investment Advisor than your violin player. Our firm prides ourselves on being the best Registered Investment Advisory (RIA) firm possible. We study constantly. We read all of the research and studies. We go to conferences and classes. And yet, no matter how hard we work, we are still your Registered Investment Advisor, and that's just *one* of the BIG FOUR areas. The days of "Jack of All Trades and Master of None" have gone by the wayside. Our firm is balanced with professionals in all four of the key areas of retirement planning: Investment, Insurance, Tax, and Legal.

In this new ever changing, complex, and volatile world, a successful retirement plan demands a consistent planning approach with all parts of the overall plan working together. You might have a fantastic insurance agent and a solid investment advisor, but if you don't also have a skilled tax advisor and legal counsel on your team, you could be losing significant chunks of your savings, which ought to be ensuring your safe, lifetime income and a legacy for your loved ones.

A great violinist is one thing, but just think of the depth and power when you add in the whole symphony. Your retirement should be symphonic.

Introduction and Client Discovery

Second Opinion Review

Present Personal Customized Blueprint

Initial Plan Implementation

Plan Tracking and Continuous Monitoring

Periodic Plan Reviews and Revisions

You are the center of our process.

The Big 4 at Jones & Associates Premier Financial Solutions, LLC

From the beginning, the foundation of Jones & Associates was based on this philosophy. We are committed to, and passionate about, one crucial mission: offering efficient and comprehensive solutions for our client's needs. We accomplish our mission through open communication and a team approach. Our Investment, Insurance, Tax, and Legal team members use transparent, strategic planning to place our client at the center throughout the entire planning and servicing process.

Using the Big 4 approach, we serve our clients in a fiduciary capacity. What's that, you ask? Excellent question. Fiduciary capacity is simply a fancy way of saying we're on each client's team. We pledge to give our clients advice based solely on their best interests. This is a critical distinction because, when choosing who will help create your retirement plan, you absolutely need to know from whom you're getting your advice and how they get paid. Brokers, for example, make a commission when they sell you a stock or mutual fund, regardless of the performance of that stock or mutual fund. RIAs, on the other hand, earn a fee based on the amount of assets under management. The incentive is to grow the portfolio so both the firm and the client win.

This is not to say anything bad about brokers (Hi, Dad! I love you!). My wife Kelly Jones is our CFO at Jones & Associates, and her father works in the industry, too. That's why, at Jones & Associates, we're not just a team. We're a family. Our clients become part of that family as well.

Jones & Associates is also part of the community. We're based in the Rogue Valley, where we not only help our clients reach their retirement goals, but also help build a stronger community as well. That's because we believe teamwork makes the dream work and this approach is the best approach everywhere: at home, at work, in retirement and throughout the community.

A Second Opinion Should Be Your First Priority

Even if you already have a financial advisor or team, we would love to invite you to come and visit with us. Remember, we can all count on a longer life these days. Congratulations! According to the Social Security Administration, Americans live, on average, approximately 20 years into retirement.* You want to enjoy all of those years. Retirement is no time for skimping and worrying.

---

*http://www.ssa.gov/planners/lifeexpectancy.htm

You've worked your whole life, and retirement should be your reward. It's our goal to make sure that is exactly what happens.

To ensure that every person has the best possible retirement plan, we offer completely free second opinions. Come in and sit with us. We'll learn about you, your retirement goals, your hopes and dreams and your current financial situation, just as we do with every client who comes through our doors. We will analyze all of your current investments and financial accounts, and then... we'll tell you the truth. If that sounds surprising, well, that's because maybe it is. We're not here to take your business away from anyone. If you've already got a fantastic team working for you with all of the Big 4 in place, you might have a financial plan that will last a lifetime. That's exactly what we'll tell you. If there is any way we can improve your financial plan, we'll tell you that too.

If you decide to become part of the Jones & Associates family, the next step will be crafting a custom retirement plan based on your situation, goals and needs. The process goes like this:

Organize your assets. Organize your finances, assets, obligations, and liabilities, and make them simple to understand. This can start with a simple list of the financial solutions(s) you own and a list of your debts and other obligations. A financial professional will help you sort out the value of each asset, the beneficiaries that are listed for each one, and how much risk each asset is exposed to. That last component, the risk assessment, will play a very important role in how you structure your retirement plan. Your financial professional may also be able to help structure your plan so that you can retire your debts and other obligations.

Create an income plan. The first thing you'll need on day one of your retirement is a reliable income. When your paycheck stops coming in, you still need to pay the bills. Understanding how much income you need each month and where it will come from will form the foundation for the rest of your retirement.

Accumulation. After your income needs are met, you have the opportunity to take your additional assets and leverage them for profit to provide you with income in the future, to prepare for anticipated health care costs, and to contribute to your legacy.

Taxes. Understanding how taxes affect your retirement income and accounts will help you make decisions that can save you money and protect your legacy.

Creating a Legacy. Creating a lasting legacy requires making smart financial decisions. Taking inventory of your assets with a professional will help ensure that your listed beneficiaries are up to date, that you have a strategy for covering health care costs, funeral expenses, and strategies for avoiding costly probate proceedings and tax penalties.

Finding a Financial Professional. Working with a financial services professional to craft your retirement is one of the smartest decisions you can make. The peace of mind that comes with working with someone you can trust who knows what solutions are available and which ones may be appropriate for you is invaluable. Choose a professional to work with who understands your needs and can connect you to the resources you need.

You will want to work with a professional who has experience in:
- IRA/401(k)/403(b) rollovers
- Asset protection
- Income planning
- Wealth management
- Long-term care solutions
- Insurance
- Estate planning
- Wealth transfer strategies

The information you've read in the introduction to this book may have already changed your view on retirement. The information in the ensuing chapters can change your approach to life in retirement by giving you confidence, knowledge, and most importantly, *control* over your retirement.

This book will address your entire financial situation from four perspectives: INVESTMENT, INSURANCE, TAX, and LEGAL.

Plan well, live well. Enjoy!

1

ORGANIZE YOUR ASSETS

"… to me, retirement means doing what you have fun doing."
– Dick Van Dyke

Marilyn and James love roller coasters. Forty-five years ago, they rode the Big Dipper at Janzten Beach Amusement Park when they honeymooned in Portland, and they were hooked. Their dream is to tour the United States when they retire. Marilyn is 63 and James is 64. They put a map of the U.S. on their bedroom wall and started marking all of the places they wanted to visit, all the classic and famous roller coasters they wanted to ride.

But then, an altogether different roller coaster hit. Both Marilyn and James had been longtime participants in their companies' 401(k) programs. They weren't sure exactly how much money they would need to retire, but they felt good about their savings. One day, though, their 401(k) accounts took a big drop. The next day, the market was up a bit, but two days later, it dropped even further. Suddenly, their once-healthy retirement savings were beginning to look frighteningly endangered.

"But what about Social Security?" James pointed out. "We'll surely have enough after Social Security."

Marilyn wasn't too sure. "Even with Social Security, we'll have to take money out of our retirement accounts to pay all of our bills. How do we take money out of our 401(k)s anyway? And how do we know we have enough money to last the rest of our lives?"

They decided it was time to find some help.

Marilyn and James aren't alone. They know they have some assets, but they aren't sure how much is enough. Their situation is made even more complicated by the fact that they are closing in on their desired retirement age, but they aren't sure what steps to take to secure the savings they have put away. As the volatile stock market eats away at their hard-earned savings, they become more and more nervous every day.

There are more questions Marilyn and James need to answer. For example:

- How will they pay for healthcare during retirement, and how does Medicare work?
- Is there a way to transfer their 401(k)s into financial solutions that aren't so exposed to market risk?
- What taxes will they owe on their retirement savings, and when will those taxes be due?
- How much income do they need each month to live comfortably?

Those questions are just the beginning. Remember, this is the new world of retirement, and it's a complex and constantly changing world. Right now, Marilyn and James are in a lifeboat. They're on their own, hoping that they've put away enough supplies, food and water to make it to shore. Sure, maybe they will make it. But retirement shouldn't be about hoping you make it to shore. Retirement should be less like surviving on a lifeboat and more like basking in the sun on a yacht. In order to sail that yacht (and allow you to bask in the sun), you need a team of experts. You need people who are great sailors, navigators, and planners. In the same way, the best possible retirement requires a team of experts as well.

Leaving your retirement up to chance is unadvisable by nearly any standard, yet millions of people find themselves *hoping* instead of planning for a happy ending. With information, tools and professional guidance, creating a successful retirement plan can put you in control of your financial management.

While you may have built up a 401(k), an IRA, and Social Security benefits, do you know what your financial picture really looks like?

Structuring assets to create an income-generating retirement requires a different approach than earning income via the workforce. Saving money for retirement, which is what you have spent your life doing, and *planning* your retirement are two different things. Both are important. Earning and saving money is different than creating a financial strategy that accounts for your income needs in retirement. Add the complexities of taxes, required minimum distributions (RMDs) from IRAs and legacy planning, and you can begin to see why happy endings require more than hope. They need a focused and well-executed plan.

Now that you know there's more to saving and planning for retirement than filing for your Social Security benefit and drawing income from your 401(k), you can begin to **create a strategy for your retirement** that can have a significant impact on your financial landscape after you stop drawing a paycheck. Creating a plan to manage your assets requires risk management, risk diversification, tax planning, income planning and legal advice throughout your life stages—a series of tasks best conquered by a communicating, cohesive team. These strategies can help you leverage more from each one of the hard-earned dollars you set aside for your retirement.

Some people file for Social Security on day one of their retirement. Others rely on supplemental income from an IRA or another retirement account. Working with a retirement team can help you determine your best course of action.

NEW IDEAS FOR RETIREMENT

As we discussed earlier, retirement has changed: the traditional sources of income and saving are no longer available or, if they're

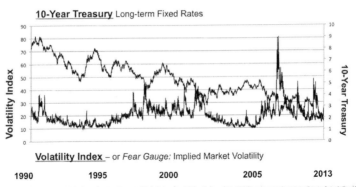

10-Year Treasury Long-term Fixed Rates

Volatility Index

Volatility Index – or *Fear Gauge:* Implied Market Volatility

1990   1995   2000   2005   2013

Source: Yahoo Finance – 12-31-2013. VIX is a trademarked ticker symbol for the Chicago Board Options Exchange Market Volatility Index, a popular measure of the implied volatility of S&P 500 index options. Often referred to as the fear index or the fear gauge, it represents one measure of the market's expectation of stock market volatility over the next 30 day period (wikipedia.com) The CBOE 10-year Treasury Note (TNX) is based on 10 times the yield-to-maturity on the most recently auctioned 10-year Treasury note. Past performance does not guarantee future results. Some illustrations may show how a market index has performed. An investor cannot invest in an index, although there are some investments designed to mirror index performance. Past performance is not a guarantee of future results.

The VIX, or volatility index, of the market represents expected market volatility. When the VIX drops, economic experts expect less volatility. When the VIX rises, more volatility is expected.

1. *VIX is a trademarked ticker symbol for the Chicago Board Options Exchange (CBOE) Market Volatility Index, a popular measure of the implied volatility of S&P 500 index options. Often referred to as the fear index or the fear gauge, it represents one measure of the market's expectation of stock market volatility over the next 30 day period. (wikipedia.com)*

2. *The CBOE 10-Year Treasury Note (TNX) is based on 10 times the yield-to-maturity on the most recently auctioned 10-year Treasury note.*

still around, they may no longer be as safe and effective as they were in the past. The market has also changed: new volatility means that the market, and your investment portfolio with it, experience sharp and frequent ups and downs. The days of slow, steady growth are gone.

Just as the retirement planning world has changed, so has the advice that goes along with it. Advice about what to do with money has been around as long as money has existed. Hindsight allows us to see which advice was good and which advice didn't cut the mustard. Some sources of advice have been around for a very long time. While there are some basic investment concepts that have stood the test of time, most strategies that work adapt to changing conditions in the market, in the economy and the world, as well as changes in your personal circumstances.

The reality is that investment strategies and savings plans that worked in the past have encountered challenging new circumstances that have turned them on their heads. The Great Recession of the early 2000s highlighted how old investment ideas were not only ineffective but incredibly destructive to the retirement plans of millions of Americans. The dawn of an entirely restructured health care system brings with it new options and challenges that will undoubtedly change the way insurance companies provide investment solutions and services.

Perhaps the most important lessons investors learned from the Great Recession is that not understanding where your money is invested (and the potential risks of those investments) can work against you, your plans for retirement and your legacy. Saving and investing money isn't enough to truly get the most out of it. You must have a planful approach to managing your assets.

Essentially, managing your money and your investments is an ongoing process that requires customization and adaptation to a changing world. And make no mistake; the world is always changing. What worked for your parents or even your parents'

parents was probably good advice back then. People in retirement or approaching retirement today need new ideas and professional guidance.

HOPE SO VS. KNOW SO MONEY

Let's take a look at some of the basic truths about money as it relates to saving for retirement.

There are essentially two kinds of money: *Hope So* and *Know So*. Everyone can divide their money into these two categories. Some have more of one kind than the other. The goal isn't to eliminate one kind of money but to balance them as you approach retirement.

Hope So Money is money that is at risk. It fluctuates with the market. It has no minimum guarantee. It is subject to investor activity, stock prices, market trends, buying trends, etc. You get the picture. This money is exposed to more risk but also has the potential for more reward. Because the market is subject to change, you can't really be sure what the value of your investments will be worth in the future. You can't really *rely* on it at all. For this reason, we refer to it as Hope So Money. This doesn't mean you shouldn't have some money invested in the market, but it would be dangerous to assume you can know what it will be worth in the future.

Hope So Money is an important element of a retirement plan, especially in the early stages of planning when you can trade volatility for potential returns, and when a longer investment timeframe is available to you. In the long run, time can smooth out the ups and downs of money exposed to the market. Working with a professional and leveraging a long-term investment strategy has the potential to create rewarding returns from Hope So Money.

Know So Money, on the other hand, is safer when compared to Hope So Money. Know So Money is made up of dependable, low-risk or no-risk money, and investments that you can count on. Social Security is one of the most common forms of Know So Money. Income you draw or will draw from Social Security is guaranteed. You have paid into Social Security your entire career, and you can rely on that money during your retirement. Unlike the market, rates of growth for Know So Money are dependent on 10-year treasury rates. The 10-year treasury, or TNX, is commonly considered to represent a very secure and safe place for your money, hence Know So Money. The 10-year treasury drives key rates for things such as mortgage rates or CD rates. Know So Money may not be as exciting as Hope So Money, but it is safer. You can safely be fairly sure you will have it in the future.

Knowing the difference between Hope So and Know So Money is an important step towards a successful retirement plan. People who are 55 or older and who are looking ahead to retirement should be relying on more Know So Money than Hope So Money.

Ideally, the rates of return on Hope So and Know So Money would have an overlapping area that provided an acceptable rate of risk for both types of money. In the early 1990s, interest rates were high and market volatility was low. At that time, you could invest in either Hope So or Know So Money options because the rates of return were similar from both Know So and Hope So investments, and you were likely to be fairly successful with a wide range of investment options. At that time, you could expose yourself to an acceptable amount of risk or an acceptable fixed rate. Basically, it was difficult to make a mistake during that time period. Today, you don't have those options. Market volatility is at all-time highs while interest rates are at all-time lows. They are so far apart from each other that it is hard to know what to do with your money.

Yesterday's investment rules may not work today. Not only could they hamper achieving your goals, they may actually harm your financial situation. We are currently in a period when the rates for Know So Money options are at historic lows, and the volatility of Hope So Money is higher than ever. There is no overlapping acceptable rate, making both options less than ideal. *Because of this uncertain financial landscape, wise investment strategies are more important now than ever.*

This unique situation requires fresh ideas and investment tools that haven't been relied on in the past. Investing the way your parents did will not pay off. The majority of investment ideas used by financial professionals in the 1990s aren't applicable to today's markets. That kind of investing will likely get you in trouble and compromise your retirement. Today, you need a different PLAN.

HOW MUCH RISK ARE YOU EXPOSED TO?

Many investors don't know how much risk they are exposed to. It is helpful to organize your assets so you can have a clear understanding of how much of your money is at risk and how much is in safer holdings. This process starts with listing all your assets.

Let's take a look at the two kinds of money:

Hope So Money is, as the name indicates, money that you *hope* will be there when you need it. Hope So Money represents what you would like to get out of your investments. Examples of Hope So Money include:

- Stock market funds, including index funds
- Mutual funds
- Variable annuities
- REITS

Know So Money is money that you know you can count on. It is safer money that isn't exposed to the level of volatility as the asset types noted above. You can more confidently count on having this money when you need it.

Examples of Know So Money are:
- Government backed bonds
- Savings and checking accounts
- Fixed income annuities
- CDs
- Treasuries
- Money market accounts

» *Terry started a brokerage account when he was 32. His father had invested in stocks and done pretty well, and Terry was excited to enjoy the same benefits. Over the years, Terry's account had performed reasonably well, but recently, it's taken a couple of frightening dips. Terry, who is now 59, also recently changed jobs. His sister Angela took him out to dinner to celebrate his new job.*

"What did you decide to do with your 401(k)?" Angela asked.

Terry hadn't even considered it. Fortunately, his sister Angela had recently met with her own financial team, and she knew what to do. But first she laughed at her big brother.

"You're the guy who won't let anyone else in the house even LOOK at the remote control, but you're going to let your former employers have control of your retirement savings?"

Angela introduced Terry to her financial team, and then Terry sat down with the team's investment advisor. She advised him to transfer his 401(k) assets into an IRA. "But," she pointed out. "Nearly every dollar you've saved for retirement is subject to market risk." She and Terry went through a list of his assets, and she explained the risk each asset faced. "It might be time to consider shifting some of your assets to a safer alternative, as you get closer to retirement."

Terry couldn't agree more.

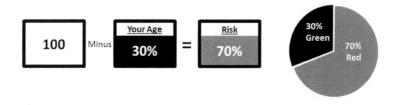

RULE OF 100

Determining the amount of risk that is right for you is dependent on a number of variables. You need to feel comfortable with where and how you are investing your money, and your financial team is obligated to help you make decisions that put your money in places that fit your risk criteria.

Your retirement needs to first accommodate your day-to-day income needs. How much money do you need to maintain your lifestyle? When do you need it?

Managing your risk by having a balance of Hope So Money vs. Know So Money is a good start that will put you ahead of the curve. But how much Know So Money is enough to secure your income needs during retirement, and how much Hope So Money is enough to allow you to continue to benefit from an improving market?

In short, how do you begin to know how much risk you should be exposed to?

When looking for a financial team, you want to work with a firm that not only offers a team approach to all of the Big 4 retirement factors, but you also want a team that approaches each retirement plan individually. Your personality, retirement dreams and financial situation are unique to you and your life. That's why it's necessary for your financial team to get to know you before considering any investment, tax, legal or insurance solutions. Risk tolerance is no different. There is no cookie cutter approach to risk tolerance. How you feel about risk is singular to you. But, there are some useful guidelines to help you understand risk. One of those guidelines is called *The Rule of 100*, and it helps demonstrate the relationship between risk and age. Our team uses the Rule of 100 as a general guideline, not as a steadfast rule. This is because every client's situation is different.

The average investor needs to accumulate assets to create a retirement plan that provides income during retirement and also allows for legacy planning. To accomplish this, they need to balance the amount of risk to which they are exposed. Risk is required because, while Know So Money is safer, more reliable and more dependable, it doesn't grow very fast, if at all. Today's historically low interest rates barely break even with current inflation. Hope So Money, while less dependable, has more potential for growth. Hope So Money can eventually become Know So Money once you move it to an investment with lower risk. Everyone's risk diversification will be different depending on their goals, age and their existing assets.

So how do you decide how much risk your assets should be exposed to? Where do you begin? Luckily, there's a guideline you can use to start making decisions about risk management. It's called the Rule of 100.

THE RIGHT RISK FOR YOU

The Rule of 100 is a general rule that helps shape asset diversification* for the average investor. The rule states that the number 100

Asset Diversification disclosure – Diversification and asset allocation does not assure or guarantee better performance and cannot eliminate the risk of investment loss. Before investing, you should carefully read the applicable volatility disclosure for each of the underlying funds, which can be found in the current prospectus.

minus an investor's age equals the percentage of assets they should have exposed to risk.

The Rule of 100: 100 - (your age) = the percentage of your assets that should be exposed to risk (Hope So Money).

For example, if you are a 30-year-old investor, the Rule of 100 would indicate that you should be focusing on investing primarily in the market and taking on a substantial amount of risk in your portfolio. The Rule of 100 suggests that 70 percent of your investments should be exposed to risk.

$$100 - (30 \text{ years of age}) = 70 \text{ percent}$$

Now, not every 30-year-old should have exactly 70 percent of their assets in mutual funds and stocks. The Rule of 100 is based on your chronological age, not your "financial age," which could vary based on your investment experience, your aversion or acceptance of risk and other factors. While this rule isn't an ironclad solution to anyone's finances, it's a pretty good place to start. Once you've taken the time to look at your assets with a professional to determine your risk exposure, you can use the Rule of 100 to make changes that put you in a more stable investment position — one that reflects your comfort level.

Perhaps when you were age 30 and starting your career, like in the example above, it made sense to have 70 percent of your money in the market: you had time on your side. You had plenty of time to save more money, work more and recover from a downturn in the market. Retirement was ages away, and your earning power was increasing. And indeed, younger investors should take on more risk for exactly those reasons. The potential reward of long-term involvement in the market outweighs the risk of investing when you are young.

Risk tolerance generally reduces as you get older, however. If you are 40 years old and lose 30 percent of your portfolio in a market downturn this year, you have 20 or 30 years to recover it. If you are 68 years old, you have five to 10 years (or less) to make the same recovery. That new circumstance changes your whole retirement perspective. At age 68, it's likely that you simply aren't as interested in suffering through a tough stock market. There is less time to recover from downturns, and the stakes are higher. The money you have saved is money you will soon need to provide you with income, or is money that you already need to meet your income demands.

Much of the flexibility that comes with investing earlier in life is related to *compounding*. Compounded earnings can be incredibly powerful over time. The longer your money has time to compound, the greater your wealth will be. This is what most people talk about when they refer to putting their money to work. This is also why the Rule of 100 favors risk for the young. If you start investing when you are young, you can invest smaller amounts of money in a more aggressive fashion because you have the potential to make a profit in a rising market and you can harness the power of compounding earnings. When you are 40, 50 or 60 years old, that potential becomes less and less and you are forced to have more money at lower amounts of risk to realize the same returns. **It basically becomes more expensive to prudently invest the older you get.**

You risk not having a recovery period the older you get, so should have less of your assets at risk in volatile investments. You should shift with the Rule of 100 to protect your assets and ensure that they will provide you with the income you need in retirement. Let's look at another example that illustrates how the Rule of 100 becomes more critical as you age. An 80-year-old investor who is retired and is relying on retirement assets for income, for example, needs to depend on a solid amount of Know So Money. The Rule of 100 says an 80-year-old investor should have a maximum of 20 percent of his or her assets at risk. Depending on the investor's financial position, even less risk exposure may be required. You are the only person who can make this kind of determination, but the Rule of 100 can help. Everyone has their own level of comfort. Your Rule of 100 results will be based on your values and attitudes as well as your comfort with risk.

The Rule of 100 can apply to overarching financial management and to specific investments as well. Take the 401(k) for example. Many people have them, but not many people understand how their money is allocated within their 401(k). An employer may have someone who comes in once a year and explains the models and options that employees can choose from, but that's as much guidance as most 401(k) holders get. Many 401(k) options include target date funds that change their risk exposure over time, essentially following a form of the Rule of 100. Selecting one of these options can often be a good move for employees because they shift your risk as you age, securing more Know So Money when you need it.

A financial professional can look at your assets with you and discuss alternatives to optimize your balance between Know So and Hope So Money.

CHAPTER 1 RECAP //

- There is money you hope you'll have in the future, and there's money you know you'll have in the future. Make sure you know how much you need when you retire.
- Organizing your assets starts with making a list. You can then understand how each asset is balanced for risk.
- Your exposure to risk is ultimately determined by you.
- Use the Rule of 100 as a general guiding principle when determining how much risk your retirement investments should be exposed to (100 - [your age] = [percentage of your investments that can comfortably exposed to risk])

2

HEED THE TRAFFIC LIGHT

Traffic lights are wonderful when they're green, a little scary when they turn yellow right when you go through them, and kind of a bummer when they're red. They also make the perfect way to look at your money as well. You're probably surprised to read that, but it's true. Using the familiar green, yellow and red labels, we can organize your investments and assets visually, making it easier to see how your assets are allocated.

We assign colors—red, yellow and green—to the different kinds of money and their level of risk. For our purposes, "Hope So Money" (which is exposed to risk and fluctuates with the market) is red money. Yellow money is actively and professionally managed money with calculated market risk, keeping the client's goals and objectives in mind. We will specifically talk about yellow money in chapter eight, as it is very important. "Know So Money" (which is more dependable) is green money. A financial professional can help you better understand the color of the money in your investment portfolio.

The fact of the matter is that a lot of people don't know their level of exposure to risk. Visually organizing your assets is an important and powerful way to get a clear picture of what kind of money you have, where it is and how you can best use it in the future. This process is as simple as listing your assets and assigning them a color based on their status as Know So or Hope So Money. Work with your financial professional to create a comprehensive inventory of your assets to understand what you are working with before making any decisions. This may be the first time you have ever sat down and sorted out all of your assets, allowing you to see how much money you have at risk in the market. Comparing the color of your investments will give you an idea of how near or far you are from adhering to the Rule of 100.

Over the course of your lifetime, it is likely that you have acquired a variety of assets. Assets can range from money that you have in a savings account or a 401(k), to a pension or an IRA. You have earned money and have made financial decisions based on the best information you had at the time. When viewed as a whole, however, you might not have an overall strategy for the management of your assets. As we have seen, it's more important than ever to know which of your assets are at risk. High market volatility and low treasury rates make for challenging financial topography. Navigating this financial landscape starts with planful asset management that takes into account your specific needs and options.

Even if you feel that you have plenty of money in your 401(k) or IRA, not knowing how much *risk* those investments are exposed to can cause you major financial suffering. Take the market crash of 2008 for example. In 2008, the average investor lost 30 percent of their 401(k). If more people had shifted their investments away from risk as they neared retirement age (i.e. the Rule of 100), they may have lost a lot less money going into retirement.

When using the Rule of 100 to calculate your level of risk, your financial age might be different than your chronological age, however. The way you organize your assets depends on your goals and your level of comfort with risk. Whatever you determine the appropriate amount of risk for you to be, you will need to organize your portfolio to reflect your goals. If you have more Red Money than Green Money, in particular, you will need to make decisions about how to move it. You can work with a financial professional to find appropriate Green Money options for your situation.

The next step is to know the right amount and ratio of Green and Red Money for you at your stage of retirement planning. In chapter eight, you will see how converting red money to yellow money can increase the overall efficiency of your retirement portfolio.

Investing heavily in Red Money and gambling all of your assets on the market is incredibly risky no matter where you fall within the Rule of 100. Money in the market can't be depended on to generate income, and a plan that leans too heavily on Red Money can easily fail, especially when investment decisions are influenced by emotional reactions to market downturns and recoveries. Not only is this an unwise plan, it can be incredibly stressful to an investor who is gambling everything on stocks and mutual funds.

But a plan that uses too much Green Money avoids all volatility and can also fail. Why? Investing all of your money in Certificates of Deposit (CDs), savings accounts, money markets and other low return accounts may provide interest and income, but that likely won't be enough to keep pace with inflation. If you focus exclusively on income from Green Money and avoid owning any stocks or mutual funds in your portfolio, you won't be able to leverage the potential for long-term growth your portfolio needs to stay healthy and productive. This is where the Rule of 100 can help you determine how much of your money should be invested in the market to anticipate your future needs.

Green Money becomes much more important as you age. While you want to reduce the amount of Red Money you have and to transition it to Green Money, you don't necessarily need all of it to generate income for you right away. Taking a closer look at Green Money, you will see there are actually different types.

TYPES OF GREEN MONEY:
NEED NOW AND NEED LATER
Money that you need to depend on for income is Green Money. Once you have filled the income gap at the beginning of your retirement, you may have money left over.

There are two types of Green Money: money used for income and money used for accumulation to meet your income needs in five, ten or twenty years. Money needed for income is Need Now Money. It is money you need to meet your basic needs, to pay your bills, your mortgage if you have one and the costs associated with maintaining your lifestyle. Money used for accumulation is Need Later Money. It's money that you don't need now for income, but will need to rely on down the road. It's still Green Money because you will rely on it later for income and will need to count on it being there. Need Later Money represents income your assets will need to generate for future use. When planning your retirement, it is vital to decide how much of your assets to structure for income and how much to set aside to accumulate in order to create Need Later Money.

You must figure out if your income and accumulation needs are met. Your Need Now and Need Later Money are top priorities. Need Now Money, in particular, will dictate what your options for future needs are.

OPTIMIZING RISK AND FINDING THE RIGHT BALANCE

Determining the amount of risk that is right for you depends on your specific situation. It starts by examining your particular financial position.

The Rule of 100 is a useful way to begin to deliberate the right amount of risk for you. But remember, it's just a baseline. Use it as a starting point for figuring out where your money should be. If you're a 50-year-old investor, the Rule of 100 suggests that you have 50 percent Green Money and 50 percent Red Money. Most 50-year-olds are more risk tolerant, however. There are many reasons why someone might be more risk tolerant, not the least of which is feeling young! Experienced investors, people who feel they need to gamble for a higher return, or people who have met their retirement income goals and are looking for additional ways to accumulate wealth are all candidates for investment strategies that incorporate higher levels of risk. In the end, it comes down to your personal tolerance for risk. How much are you willing to lose?

Consulting with a financial professional is often the wisest approach to calculating your risk level. A professional can help determine your risk tolerance by getting to know you, asking you a set of questions and even giving you a survey to determine your comfort level with different types of risk. Here's a typical scenario a financial professional might pose to you:

"You have $100,000 saved that you would like to invest in the market. There is an investment solution that could turn your $100,000 into $120,000. That same option, however, has the potential of losing you up to $30,000, leaving you with $70,000."

Is that a scenario that you are willing to enter into? Or are you more comfortable with this one:

"You could turn your $100,000 into $110,000, but have the potential of losing $15,000, leaving you with $85,000."

Your answer to these and other types of questions will help a financial professional determine what level of risk is right for you. They can then offer you investment strategies and management plans that reflect your financial age. At our firm, we call this a **customized financial blueprint**. We design this for each prospective client.

THE NUMBERS DON'T LIE

When the rubber meets the road, the numbers dictate your options. Your risk tolerance is an important indicator of what kinds of investments you should consider, but if the returns from those investments don't meet your retirement goals, your income needs will likely not be met. For example, if the level of risk you are comfortable with manages your investments at a 4 percent return and you need to realize an 8 percent return, your income needs aren't going to be met when you need to rely on your investments for retirement income. A professional may encourage you to be more aggressive with your investment strategy by taking on more risk in order to give you the potential of earning a greater return. If taking more risk isn't an option that you are comfortable with, then the discussion will turn to how you can earn more money or spend less in order to align your needs with your resources more closely.

How are you going to structure your income flow during retirement? The answer to this question dictates how you determine your risk tolerance. If the numbers say that you need to be more aggressive with your investing, or that you need to modify your lifestyle, it becomes a choice you need to make.

WORKING WITH A FINANCIAL PROFESSIONAL

Take a moment to think about your income goals:

What is your lifestyle today? Would you like to maintain it into retirement? Are you meeting your needs? Are you happy with your lifestyle? What do you really *need* to live on when you retire?

Some people will have the luxury of maintaining or improving their lifestyle, while others may have to make decisions about what they need versus what they want during their retirement.

Organizing your assets, understanding the color of your money, and creating an income and accumulation plan for retirement can quickly become an overwhelming task. The fact of the matter is that financial professionals build their careers around understanding the different variables affecting retirement financing.

Working with a Registered Investment Advisory Firm means working with a professional who is legally obligated to help you make financial decisions that are in your best interest and fall within your comfort zone. Taking steps toward creating a retirement plan is nothing to take lightly. By leveraging tax strategies, properly organizing your assets, and accumulating helpful financial solutions that help you meet your income and accumulation needs, you are more likely to meet your goals. You might have a million dollars socked away in a savings account, but your neighbor, who has $300,000 in a diverse investment portfolio that is tailored to their needs, may end up enjoying a better retirement lifestyle. Why? They had more than a good work ethic and a penchant for saving. They had a planful approach to retirement asset allocation.

CHAPTER 2 RECAP //

- There are three types of money: Red, Yellow, and Green. Red Money represents assets that are exposed to risk. Yellow money represents assets that are professionally and actively managed money with calculated market risk, keeping clients' goals and objectives in mind. Green Money represents assets that are more reliable.
- There are two types of Green Money: *Need Now and Need Later.* It is important to structure your investments to provide you with income now and later.
- Working with a Registered Investment Advisory Firm will help you compose a clear and concise inventory of your assets, and learn how much they are worth, what rules apply to them, and how they are structured for risk.
- A Registered Investment Advisory Firm can help you structure your investments so as to reflect your risk tolerance.
- Working with an Investment Advisor means working with a professional who is legally obligated to help you make financial decisions that are in your best interest and fall within your comfort zone.

3

CREATE A RETIREMENT INCOME PLAN

You deserve a worry-free retirement. That requires planning ahead, and an important aspect of your retirement financial plan is identifying your income needs. Once you have a solid understanding of how much income you'll need in retirement, you'll have a much better idea of how much of your savings you need to structure for income and how much you can set aside for growth.

During the years you are working, the main financial goal is, of course, to pay your bills but also to save as much as possible. But once you retire, your financial strategy changes. Retirement isn't about sitting back and spending all of that money you spent your working days putting away. Your savings are actually more like seeds. When you retire, you want to work with a financial professional who can help you plant your seeds in the ideal soil:

some of that soil will protect your seed and provide long, safe growth. That's the income you will live on right now. You might also want to plant some of your seeds in supercharged soil that will make your money grow faster, generating additional income for the future.

LIFE HAPPENS

You might imagine retirement as a permanent vacation, but without the right plan in place, even the most robust of savings can dwindle. Our goal is to help our clients achieve whatever retirement dreams they might have, and that requires actively managing a retirement income strategy and having the right advisor. That's because, as you already know, life happens. Things can pop up suddenly and change all of your best-laid plans. Health issues can arise, or perhaps the need for a new car. Your roof suddenly springs a leak or perhaps you want to help with your grandchild's tuition or take your family on a vacation. The point is that, especially in this new economic world, one thing is absolutely certain: change. This is why it's more necessary than ever to have a retirement team to help you create a retirement income plan and adjust that plan whenever challenges or changes arise.

If you're not feeling financially prepared, you're not alone. The market decline of 2008 hit a lot of people pretty hard. The Urban Institute's report "How Is the Financial Crisis Affecting Retirement Savings?" revealed exactly how hard. According to the report, retirement account assets, held in defined contribution plans and IRAs, reached $8.9 trillion on September 30, 2007, with about 70 percent of these assets invested in stocks. As of August 31, 2009, retirement accounts had dropped $2.3 trillion, losing 26 percent of their value.* For those people who were nearing retirement but not quite there, that loss hit particularly hard,

---

*http://www.urban.org/publications/901283.html

slashing their retirement savings so close to the time when they had hoped to start using them.

These statistics underscore how crucial a proper retirement plan is today. It has never been more important to have both a plan in place and a financial professional who can help you adjust that plan whenever challenges arise.

HOW MUCH IS RIGHT?

Lewis came in to Jones & Associates with one question: how much is right? He wanted to know a specific number: how much income he should plan for, how much of his savings should be kept safe and how much should be exposed to risk. Lewis was a biologist, and he believed in precision. He planned to apply that same precision to his retirement: determine the right formula, follow it and get results.

*Lewis was a little disappointed to discover that no such formula exists. The good news, however, was that he came to the right place. After all, there isn't ONE formula for retirement success, but our job is to create a custom formula for each of our clients. That's exactly what we did for Lewis. We call this a **customized financial blueprint**.*

The general rule of thumb is that you'll need 70-80 percent of your pre-retirement income to maintain your current lifestyle in retirement. But for Lewis, things were a bit different. Lewis had a longtime dream of traveling the United States in search of a long list of creatures he had always wanted to observe in the wild. That trip, which might take years, was the central goal of his retirement plan. As such, we structured a retirement income plan that would generate 100 percent of Lewis's pre-retirement income, allowing him to maintain his home and regular bills while also paying for his cross-country trip.

As you can see, retirement income needs are highly personal, and they should be planned for that way. Determining your income needs requires figuring out two critical things: ***how much you need*** and ***when you will need it.***

How Much Money Do You Need? This is the potential rule-of-thumb: 70 to 80 percent of your pre-retirement income is necessary to maintain your lifestyle. Remembering our friend Lewis, consider whether you might need more than 70-80 percent. Once you have determined that number, the next step is figuring out which investment strategies, options and solutions would be right for generating that income.

When Do You Need Your Money? Certain solutions work well for generating income that will last for the next 10 years. Other solutions are good for creating income that can be used 10 years from now.

So how do you figure out how much you need and when you need it? One way to get started is to make a list of all of your current expenses and bills each month. Next, add to that list all of the unusual expenses you've encountered over the last few years. Are there any potential major expenditures coming up, such a new roof, medical tests or automobile replacement or maintenance? Finally, make a separate column for those dream expenses—things like travel, going back to school, or putting aside money for your grandchildren. A good income plan should cover all of the things you MUST pay for in retirement, but also, if possible, the things you WANT to pay for as well.

Take that list and go visit your financial professional. When you work with an advisor who specializes in retirement, that advisor can offer additional insight into expenses that tend to pop up. This is a lifetime income plan, so the goal is to plan for every potential expense. There will be plenty of unexpected expenses and changes, so having the most comprehensive plan possible to start with gives you the advantage.

Once you have a good idea of your income needs, you and your advisor can begin discussing strategies to help meet those needs. Even if you already have a retirement income plan in place—and good for you if you do!—it never hurts to get a second opinion.

Look for a financial professional who offers a free, no-obligation second opinion. After all, you've worked hard, and your retirement should be everything you dream of it being. Having the best possible advice is paramount in making that happen.

CHAPTER 3 RECAP //

- The foundation of a retirement strategy depends on knowing how much money you need and when you need it.

4

UNCOVER THE SECRETS OF SOCIAL SECURITY

At Jones & Associates, we have a lot of clients who are in their late 50s, and early 60s, since we specialize in retirement. When they come in, one of their biggest concerns, and the first thing they want to discuss, is income. Beth and Roger were no different.

» *Beth was a school teacher, 64, and her husband of 38 years, Roger, 63, worked at a marketing agency. Both of them were considering retiring in the next couple of years, but they were also new grandparents. The past few years had been full of enjoying their twin granddaughters, and suddenly, they were right at retirement's door with lots of questions. On the day they came to visit, Beth was the ready with a list of questions.*

Her most pressing worry, like many retirees, was making their savings last.

"We've been saving and saving, but I just don't understand quite how all of this money will provide us with income without running out."

The answer to Beth's question starts with a strategic retirement income plan, and that plan begins with Social Security. For nine out of 10 Americans, Social Security is the foundation of retirement income.* Like an annuity or pension, Social Security represents safe, Green Money income. As such, it makes the ideal starting point for income planning.

Whether Social Security makes up a large percentage of your income or a small one, it is still a vital source of retirement funds. It's also a complex one. There are 96 months in which you can file for Social Security. If you're married, there are 9,000 possible combinations regarding how you and your spouse can file. Add to that the many advanced filing strategies you can use, and Social Security becomes sort of like a chess game. What moves you make and when you make them can make the difference between receiving the maximum possible Social Security income and leaving thousands of dollars on the table.

Here are some facts that illustrate how Americans currently use Social Security:

- 90 percent of Americans age 65 and older receive Social Security benefits.*
- Social Security provides 39 percent of income for retired Americans.*
- Claiming Social Security benefits at the wrong time can reduce your monthly benefit by up to 57 percent.**

---

*http://www.ssa.gov/news/press/basicfact.html
**When to Claim Social Security Benefits, David Blanchett, CFA, CFP® January, 2013

- 43% of men and 48% of women claim Social Security benefits at age 62.*
- 74 percent of retirees receive reduced Social Security benefits.*
- In 2013, the average monthly Social Security benefit was $1,261. *The maximum benefit for 2013 was $2,533. The $1,272 monthly benefit reduction between the average and the maximum is applied for life.***

THE BIG DECISION

The choice you make, when selecting when and how to take your Social Security, is one of the most important decisions you will make as you plan for retirement. That's because of all the different calculations and strategies involved in filing, which, unfortunately, many people aren't even aware of. You might think, Hey! I'm 62! I've been working all my life, and now I qualify for Social Security. I'm out!

Sometimes that's a great idea. Sometimes not so much.

With all of the myriad Social Security selection options, what's a soon-to-be-retiree to do? First of all, make your decision carefully. Once you have taken your Social Security for 12 months, that decision can't be reversed. Up to 12 months, you can choose to suspend your benefits, but you have to pay back all of the payments you've received, which can be painful.

Second, seek out a financial advisor who can run a Social Security Maximization report. A proprietary software program creates this report based on all of your specific details, such as age, marital status, etc. and provides a solid basis on which to decide when you take Social Security.

---

*When to Claim Social Security Benefits, David Blanchett, CFA, CFP® January, 2013
**http://www.socialsecurity.gov/pressoffice/factsheets/colafacts2013.com

» Judy and Dorothy are next-door neighbors. They often get together in the evenings for a game of gin, and recently, they've been discussing retirement. Judy has worked full-time as a nurse her whole life, and she is excited about retiring to spend more time with her grandkids. Dorothy is a homemaker, and her husband passed away a couple of years ago, leaving a pension that cares for his wife. Dorothy, who is 67, knows she's eligible for spousal Social Security benefits, but she's not sure how to get them or how much money they would provide.

Judy will turn 62 in a month, and she has decided to file for Social Security as soon as her benefits become available. She's worried, though, about her friend Dorothy. Judy suggests that Dorothy consult a financial advisor, but Dorothy says she wouldn't even know where to begin. "And don't they ask lots of personal questions?" she asks. "I would be too shy to talk to a stranger about money."

Judy has an idea. "What if we go together? My nephew is a financial advisor, and he's a very nice young man."

A week later, Judy and Dorothy go to see Judy's nephew Steve. They explain to Steve that they would prefer to visit with him together, and so he takes them into the conference room.

After several hours of discussion, though, Aunt Judy got a surprise. Steve put all of her information into his firm's Social Security Maximization program and said, "Aunt Judy, here's the thing. If you opt to take your Social Security next month, you could potentially receive $50,000 less over your lifetime."

Judy was stunned. She had been so looking forward to retiring right away.

"Don't worry, Aunt Judy. There might be a way we can structure some of your other assets for income, so that you can put off taking Social Security until later. You've worked at

Oregon State hospital for thirty years, haven't you? I bet you have some other options we can make work for you."

Dorothy, however, got some very good news. Her husband was four years older than her, and he hadn't filed for Social Security before he passed away. His benefit was at its maximum level, and she could file for spousal benefits right away.

Social Security provides an important income foundation for hundreds of thousands of Americans, but how many Americans will receive the maximum benefit they deserve? The best way to know for sure that you are building your retirement income plan on the strongest foundation possible is to seek the help of a financial professional.

We'll go into some of the specific calculations and strategies that can make a significant difference in your Social Security payments, but first, let's cover some of the basics. This isn't a comprehensive guide to Social Security, but instead a primer to give you a basic understanding of how Social Security works and how you can make it work for you.

Eligibility. Understanding how and when you are eligible for Social Security benefits will help clarify what to expect when the time comes to claim them.

To receive retirement benefits from Social Security, you must earn eligibility. In almost all cases, Americans born after 1929 must earn 40 quarters of credit to be eligible to draw their Social Security retirement benefit. In 2013, a Social Security credit represents $1,160 earned in a calendar quarter. The number changes as it is indexed each year, but not drastically. In 2012, a credit represented $1,130. Four quarters of credit is the maximum number that can be earned each year. In 2013, an American would have had to earn at least $4,640 to accumulate four credits. In order to qualify for retirement benefits, you must earn a minimum number of credits. Additionally, if you are at least 62 years old and have been married to a recipient of Social Security benefits for at least 12 months, you can choose to receive Spousal Benefits. Although 40 is the minimum number of credits required to begin drawing benefits, it is important to know that once you claim your Social Security benefit, there is no going back. Although there may be cost of living adjustments made, you are locked into that base benefit amount forever.

Primary Insurance Amount. You can think of your Primary Insurance Amount (PIA) like a ripening fruit. It represents the amount of your Social Security benefit at your Full Retirement Age (FRA). Your benefit becomes fully ripe at your FRA, and will neither reduce nor increase due to early or delayed retirement options. If you opt to take benefits before your FRA, however, your monthly benefit will be less than your PIA. You will essentially be picking an unripened fruit. On the one hand, waiting until after your FRA to access your benefits will increase your benefit beyond your PIA. On the other hand, you don't want the fruit to overripen, because every month you wait is one less check you get from the government.

Full Retirement Age. Your FRA is an important figure for anyone who is planning to rely on Social Security benefits in their retirement. Depending on when you were born, there is a specific age at which you will attain FRA. Your FRA is dictated by your year of birth and is the age at which you can begin your full monthly benefit. Your FRA is important because it is half of the equation used to calculate your Social Security benefit. The other half of the equation is based on when you start taking benefits.

When Social Security was initially set up, the FRA was age 65, and it still is for people born before 1938. But as time has passed, the age for receiving full retirement benefits has increased. If you were born between 1938 and 1960, your full retirement age is somewhere on a sliding scale between 65 and 67. Anyone born in 1960 or later will now have to wait until age 67 for full benefits.

Increasing the FRA has helped the government reduce the cost of the Social Security program, which pays out more than a half trillion dollars to beneficiaries every year!*

While you can begin collecting benefits as early as age 62, the amount you receive as a monthly benefit will be less than it would be if you wait until you reach your FRA or surpass your FRA. It is important to note that if you file for Social Security benefits before your FRA, *the reduction to your monthly benefit will remain in place for the rest of your life.* You can also delay receiving benefits up to age 70, in which case your benefits will be higher than your PIA for the rest of your life.

At FRA, 100 percent of PIA is available as a monthly benefit.

At age 62, your Social Security retirement benefits are available. For each month you take benefits prior to your FRA, however, the monthly amount of your benefit is reduced. *This reduction stays in place for the rest of your life.*

At age 70, your monthly benefit reaches its maximum. After you turn age 70, your monthly benefit will no longer increase.

Year of Birth	Full Retirement Age
1943-1954	66
1955	66 and 2 months
1956	66 and 4 months
1957	66 and 6 months
1958	66 and 8 months
1959	66 and 10 months
1960 or later	age 67**

---

*http://www.ssa.gov/pressoffice/basicfact.htm

**http://www.ssa.gov/OACT/progdata/nra.html

ROLLING UP YOUR SOCIAL SECURITY

Your Social Security income "rolls up" the longer you wait to claim it. Your monthly benefit will continue to increase until you turn 70 years old. But because Social Security is the foundation of most people's retirement, many Americans feel that they don't have control over how or when they receive their benefits. As a matter of fact, only 4 percent of Americans wait until after their FRA to file for benefits! This trend persists, despite the fact that every dollar you increase your Social Security income by means less money you will have to spend from your nest egg to meet your retirement income needs! For many people, creating their Social Security strategy is the most important decision they can make to positively impact their retirement. *The difference between the best and worst Social Security decision can be tens of thousands of dollars over a lifetime of benefits — up to $170,000!*

Deciding NOW or LATER: Following the above logic, it makes sense to wait as long as you can to begin receiving your Social Security benefit. However, the answer isn't always that simple. Not everyone has the option of waiting. Many people need to rely on Social Security on day one of their retirement. In fact, *nearly 50 percent of 62-year-old Americans file for Social Security benefits.* Why is this number so high? Some might need the income. Others might be in poor health and don't feel they will live long enough to make FRA worthwhile for themselves or their families. It is also possible, however, that the majority of folks taking an early benefit at age 62 are simply under-informed about Social Security. Perhaps they make this major decision based on rumors and emotion.

File Immediately if You:
- Find your job is unbearable.
- Are willing to sacrifice retirement income.
- Are not healthy and need a reliable source of income.

Consider Delaying Your Benefit if You:
- Want to maximize your retirement income.
- Want to increase retirement benefits for your spouse.
- Are still working and like it.
- Are healthy and willing / able to wait to file.

So if you decide to wait, how long should you wait? Lots of people can put it off for a few years, but not everyone can wait until they are 70 years old. Your individual circumstances may be able to help you determine when you should begin taking Social Security. If you do the math, you will quickly see that between ages 62 and 70, there are 96 months in which you can file for your Social Security benefit. If you take into account those 96 months and the 96 months your spouse could also file for Social Security, the number of different strategies for structuring your benefit, you can easily end up with more than 20,000 different scenarios. It's safe to say this isn't the kind of math that most people can easily handle. Each month would result in a different benefit amount. The longer you wait, the higher your monthly benefit amount becomes. Each month you wait, however, is one less month that you receive a Social Security check.

The goal is to maximize your lifetime benefits. That may not always mean waiting until you can get the largest monthly payment. Taking the bigger picture into account, you want to find out how to get the most money out of Social Security over the number of years that you draw from it. Don't underestimate the power of optimizing your benefit: the difference between the BEST and WORST Social Security election can easily be between $30,000 to $50,000 in lifetime benefits. *The difference can be very substantial!*

If you know that every month you wait, your Social Security benefit goes up a little bit, and you also know that every month you wait, you receive one less benefit check, how do you determine where the sweet spot is that maximizes your benefits over your lifetime? Financial professionals have access to software that will calculate the best year and month for you to file for benefits based on your default life expectancy. You can further customize that information by estimating your life expectancy based on your health, habits and family history. If you can then create an income plan (we'll get into this later in the chapter) that helps you wait until the target date for you to file for Social Security, you can optimize your retirement income strategy to get the most out of your Social Security benefit. How can you calculate your life expectancy? Well, you don't know exactly how long you'll live, but you have a better idea than the government does. They rely on averages to make their calculations. *You have much more personal information about your health, lifestyle and family history than they do.* You can use that knowledge to game the system and beat all the other people who are making uninformed decisions by filing early for Social Security.

While you can and should educate yourself about how Social Security works, the reality is you don't need to know a lot of general information about Social Security in order to make choices about your retirement. What you do need to know is exactly *what to do to maximize your benefit.* Because knowing what you need to do has a huge impact on your retirement! For most Americans, Social Security is the foundation of income planning for retirement. Social Security benefits represent nearly 40 percent of the income of retirees.* For many people, it can represent the largest portion of their retirement income. Not treating your Social Security benefit as an asset and investment tool can lead to sub-optimization of your largest source of retirement income.

Let's take a look at an example that shows the impact of working with a financial professional to optimize Social Security benefits:

---

*http://www.socialsecurity.gov/pressoffice/basicfact.htm

» *Michael, 62, and Diane, 61, met 38 years ago when they were both junior employees at Harry & David. Over the years, they took advantage of every possible savings opportunity, and now they're ready to start thinking about retirement. Michael is an accountant, but Diane worked in sales. Her job allowed her to travel all across the U.S.—an opportunity she loved—and now she would love to show Michael some of her favorite places.*

They sat down with a financial professional who logged onto the Social Security website to look up their PIAs. Michael's PIA is $1,900 and Diane's is $900.

If they cash in at age 62 and begin taking retirement benefits from Social Security, they will receive an estimated $492,000 in lifetime benefits. That may seem like a lot, but if you divide that amount over 20 years, it averages out to be just shy of $25,000 per year. Michael and Diane are accustomed to a more significant annual income than that. To make up the difference, they will have to rely on alternative retirement income options. They will basically have to depend on a bigger nest egg to provide them with the income they need.

If they wait until their FRA, they will increase their lifetime benefits to an estimated $523,700. This option allows them to achieve their Primary Insurance Amount, which will provide them a $33,000 annual income.

After learning Michael and Diane's needs and using software to calculate the most optimal time to begin drawing benefits, their financial professional determined that the best option for them drastically increases their potential lifetime benefits to $660,000!

*By using strategies that their financial professional recommended, they increased their potential lifetime benefits by as much as **$148,000**. There's no telling how much you could* *miss out on from your Social Security if you don't take time to create a strategy that calculates your maximum benefit. For Michael and Diane, the value of maximizing their benefits was the difference between night and day. While this may seem like a special case, it isn't uncommon to find benefit increases of this magnitude. You'll never know unless you take a look at your own options.*

Despite the importance of knowing when and how to take your Social Security benefit, many of today's retirees and pre-retirees may know little about the mechanics of Social Security and how they can maximize their benefit.

So, to whom should you turn for advice when making this complex decision? Before you pick up the phone and call Uncle Sam, you should know that the Social Security Administration (SSA) representatives are actually prohibited from giving you election advice! Plus, SSA representatives in general are trained to focus on monthly benefit amounts, not the lifetime income for a family.

MAXIMIZING YOUR LIFETIME BENEFIT

As discussed in Chapter 2, calculating how to maximize **lifetime benefits** is more important than waiting until age 70 for your maximum **monthly benefit amount.** It's about getting the most income during your lifetime. Professional benefit maximization software can target the year and month that it is most beneficial for you to file based on your life expectancy.

The three most common ages that people associate with retirement benefits are 62 (Earliest Eligible Age), 66 (Full Retirement Age), and 70 (age at which monthly maximum benefit is reached). In almost all circumstances, however, none of those three most common ages will give you the maximum lifetime benefit.

Remember, every month you wait to file, the amount of your benefit check goes up, but you also get one less check. You don't know how exactly how long you're going to live, but you have a better idea of your life expectancy than the actuaries at the Social Security Administration who can only work with averages. They can't make calculations based on your specific situation. A professional can run the numbers for you and get the target date that maximizes your potential lifetime benefits. You can't get this information from the SSA, but you *can* get it from a financial professional.

Your Social Security options don't stop here, however. There are a plethora of other choices you can make to manipulate your benefit payments.

Just a Few Types of Social Security Benefits:
- *Retired Worker Benefit.* This is the benefit with which most people are familiar. The Retired Worker Benefit is what most people are talking about when they refer to Social Security. It is your benefit based on your earnings and the amount that you have paid into the system over the span of your career.
- *Spousal Benefit.* The Spousal Benefit is available to the spouse of someone who is eligible for Retired Worker Benefits. What if there was a way for your spouse to receive his or her benefit for four years and not lose the chance to get his or her maximum benefit when he or she turns age 70? Many people do not know about this strategy and might be missing out on benefits they have earned.
- *Survivorship Benefit.* When one spouse passes away, the survivor is able to receive the larger of the two benefit amounts.
- *File and Suspend.* This concept allows for a lower-earning spouse to receive up to 50 percent of the other's PIA amount if both spouses file for benefits at the right time.

- *Restricted Application.* A higher-earning spouse may be able to start collecting a spousal benefit on the lower-earning spouse's benefit while allowing his or her benefit to continue to grow.

THE DIVORCE FACTOR

How does a divorced spouse qualify for benefits? If you have gone through a divorce, it might affect the retirement benefit to which you are entitled.

A person can receive benefits as a divorced spouse on a former spouse's Social Security record if he or she:

- Was married to the former spouse for at least 10 years;
- Is at least age 62 years old;
- Is unmarried; and
- Is not entitled to a higher Social Security benefit on his or her own record.*

With all of the different options, strategies and benefits to choose from, you can see why filing for Social Security is more complicated than just mailing in the paperwork. Gathering the data and making yourself aware of all your different options isn't enough to know exactly what to do, however. On the one hand, you can knock yourself out trying to figure out which options are best for you and wondering if you made the best decision. On the other hand, you can work with a financial professional who uses customized software that takes all the variables of your specific situation into account and calculates your best option. You have tens of thousands of different options for filing for your Social Security benefit. If your spouse is a different age than you are, it nearly doubles the amount of options you have. This is far more complicated arithmetic than most people can do on their own.

---

*http://www.ssa.gov/retire2/yourdivspouse.htm

If you want a truly accurate understanding of when and how to file, you need someone who will ask you the right questions about your situation, someone who has access to specialized software that can crunch the numbers. The reality is that you need to work with a professional that can provide you with the sophisticated analysis of your situation that will help you make a truly informed decision.

Important Questions about Your Social Security Benefit:
How can I maximize my lifetime benefit? By knowing when and how to file for Social Security. This usually means waiting until you have at least reached your Full Retirement Age. A professional has the experience and the tools to help determine when and how you can maximize your lifetime benefits.

Who will provide reliable advice for making these decisions? Only a professional has the tools and experience to provide you reliable advice.

Will the Social Security Administration provide me with the advice? The Social Security Administration cannot provide you with advice or strategies for claiming your benefit. They can give you information about your monthly benefit, but that's it. They also don't have the tools to tell you what your specific best option is. They can accurately answer how the system works, but they can't advise you on what decision to make as to how and when to file for benefits.

The Maximization Report that your financial professional will generate represents an invaluable resource for understanding how and when to file for your Social Security benefit. When you get your customized Social Security Maximization Report, you will not only know all the options available to you—but you will understand the financial implications of each choice. In addition to the analysis, you will also get a report that shows *exactly* at what age—including which month and year—you should trigger benefits and how you should apply. It also includes a variety of other time-specific recommendations, such as when to apply for Medicare or take Required Minimum Distributions from your qualified plans. A report means there is no need to wonder, or to try to figure out when to take action – the Social Security Maximization Report lays it all out for you in plain English.

CHAPTER 4 RECAP //

- To get the most out of your Social Security benefit, you need to file at the right time.
- An Investment Advisor can help you determine when you should file for Social Security to get your Maximum Lifetime Benefit.

5

GENERATE RETIREMENT INCOME TO FILL THE GAP

During your working years, you get a pay check. That's your income. When you retire, income is no longer generated by the work you do every day, but instead by the assets you've saved during all of those working years. As we discussed in Chapter 4, Social Security is a Green Money source of money that forms the foundation of your retirement income plan. But that's just the beginning. According to the Social Security Administration, Social Security benefits provide approximately 38 percent of the income for America's retirees. That means most retirees depend on other forms of income to make up the remainder of their income needs: a shortfall that we call the Income Gap.

The Income Gap is basically the difference between your monthly Social Security benefit amount and your desired monthly income. The key to filling that Income Gap is to reposition your assets to generate enough income to eliminate that gap—using the least amount of money as possible. Your financial professional can help you find Green Money solutions that will generate enough money to cover your Income Gap with the smallest possible investment. The remainder of your assets can then be invested for growth, providing a source for your Need Later income. Take Charles and Grace, for example:

> » *Charles and Grace were both 61 years old, and retirement was starting to look very appealing. They already knew that they required $6,000 each month to cover their expenses, and at a previous meeting with their financial team, they had gotten a Social Security Maximization report that told them they would receive $4,200 every month. They had one more source of income, a small basement apartment that they rented for $350 monthly. They added all that together and discovered that they would have a $1,450 shortfall every month. They weren't sure what would be the best way to generate that income, but one thing was clear: it was time to meet with their financial team.*
>
> *Fortunately, Charles and Grace also had another asset: they had been contributing to an IRA account for many years, and its current value was $350,000. They were worried, though, about draining that account.*
>
> *"We did some of our own math," Grace told their financial advisor, "and if we take $1,450 out of our IRA every month, it will only last 20 years. Plus, it's invested in the market. What will we do if the market takes a downturn like 2008, and we lose a huge chunk of our IRA?"*

Charles chimed in too, "We looked at using some of our IRA to buy U.S. Treasury Notes, but the interest rates were so low. It just didn't seem to make much sense. Surely there are other options?"

Charles and Grace were both right. They needed a solution that would provide enough growth to offset the withdrawals they would need to make to replace their monthly shortfall; it would also need to deliver enough growth to keep ahead of inflation. Because their IRA was traditional (not Roth), they would have to pay taxes on any withdrawals they might make. A solution that provided some kind of tax advantage would also be very helpful.

Withdrawing all of their IRA and doing a Roth conversion was one option, their advisor explained, but if they removed all of that money at once, it would launch them into a tax bracket that would siphon off a significant portion of their IRA. The advisor had another idea.

"One option is to take a lump sump from your IRA and use that money to purchase a fixed index annuity with an income rider," he explained. "It's important to choose your annuity carefully, because they're not all created the same. But a fixed index annuity can provide a good solution for guaranteed income, if it's the right fit for you.

He worked with them to select the fixed index annuity that was right for their situation. They made a $249,455 lump sum IRA withdrawal and purchased a fixed index annuity with an income rider that would guarantee $1,450 of income per month. Their advisor walked them through the entire contract, making sure that every element was right for them, including things like the surrender period, fees, etc.

Their income needs taken care of, Charles and Grace still had $100,000 remaining in their IRA. They were able to *restructure their existing investments into Yellow Money that would be managed specifically for their future income needs.*

TAKING A HYBRID APPROACH TO YOUR INCOME NEEDS

You looked at Social Security strategies earlier, discovering you have some control over how and when you file. Those decisions can change the outcome of your benefit in your favor. Once you start drawing that income, it is safer and will provide you with a reliable source of income for the rest of your life. While there are many factors of Social Security that you can control, there are many that you cannot.

For example, you do not have the choice of putting more money into Social Security in order to get more out of it. If you could have the option to contribute more money toward Social Security in order to secure a guaranteed income, it would be a great way to create a Green Money asset that would enhance your retirement. Since that option isn't available, you may seek an investment tool that is similar to Social Security that provides you with a reliable income. It also has the potential to increase the value of your principal investment! This kind of win-win situation exists, and it's called an annuity.

Today, you probably have savings in a variety of assets that you acquired over the years. But you may not have taken time to examine them and assess how they will support your retirement.

It's not about whether the market goes up or down, but when it does. If it goes down at the wrong time for your five or 10-year retirement horizon, you could be in serious danger of losing some of your retirement income.

If you have assets that you would like to structure for retirement income, ***a fixed index annuity may be the right choice for you.***

HOW ANNUITIES FIT INTO AN OVERALL INCOME PLAN

Here's another unique thing about the new world of retirement: today, quite simply, there are a *lot* of people retiring. Every day 10,000 Baby Boomers turn 65 years old. What's more, Baby Boomers currently own 60 percent of all investable assets in our country.* That makes the Baby Boomers a powerful section of the population, and their influence has driven a number of new financial solutions to market. For example, annuities have been around for quite some time, but the fixed index annuity of today is a whole new idea, a hybrid of various older solutions.

Traditional annuities. These older forms of annuities offered less than favorable terms compared to today's annuities. First of all, when you bought a traditional annuity, you were giving up all access to your premium. In exchange, the insurance company would agree to pay a set lifetime income, but there was a catch. You might buy an annuity for, say, $150,000, and the insurance company would agree to pay you $1,000 each month for the rest of your life. But then you sadly and unexpectedly died in a hot air balloon accident two weeks later! What happened to your $150,000? Did your family get it? Nope. The insurance company retained every cent. Or, instead of the hot air balloon accident, let's say you simply needed that $150,000. Could you withdraw it? Once again, no. When you bought a traditional annuity, you gave up every cent of that investment. The only payback you got was that promised $1,000 of income. End of story.

Fixed index annuities. This new type of an annuity, which was introduced recently, is a hybrid, a combination of fixed annuities and variable annuities. As Baby Boomers grew older and closer to retirement, experiencing the newly volatile market all along

---

Will the Demand for Assets Fall When the Baby Boomers Retire? By Marika Santoro. Congressional Budget Office. Sept. 8, 2009.

the way, they demanded a safer option for their investments, and some insurance companies came through. Now, before we get into the details, let's underscore one more time: all fixed index annuities are not created equal. Each insurance company sells its own version of the product, with its own specific limits and rules. There could be a fixed index annuity out there that works perfectly for your situation, but, like most financial solutions, fixed index annuities aren't one-size-fits-all answers.

Fixed index annuities, as mentioned earlier, are just one of several kinds of annuities. In general, annuities come in various types, divided by how they distribute money (immediate or deferred) and how they earn interest (fixed or variable).

- *Immediate annuities.* These annuities allow you to start receiving payments immediately after you make your first payment, but often they require that you give up access to your premium.
- *Deferred annuities.* These annuities accumulate interest for a set amount of time or until you, as the owner, decide to turn yours into an immediate annuity.
- *Fixed annuities.* These annuities are guaranteed and earn money based on a set interest rate.
- *Variable annuities.* These annuities are actually a kind of security (similar to a stock, bond or mutual fund) and as such, they are not guaranteed. They earn their interest just as a security does, based on the performance of whatever mutual fund, stock or bond they're invested in.

THE HYBRID ANNUITY

Fixed index annuities are actually a hybrid of variable and fixed annuities. Instead of earning interest based on a set (fixed) interest rate, like the fixed annuity, a fixed index annuity is tied to an index, such as the Standard & Poors (S&P) 500 or the Dow Jones Industrial Average (DJIA). But unlike variable annuities, which are also tied to an index, fixed index annuities are actually guaranteed. What does that mean, guaranteed?

It's like this: in 2008, many investors took a huge loss—25 percent, or even up to 50 percent in extreme cases. But, if you had your savings in a fixed index annuity in 2008, you were one of the lucky people who lost nothing. You also gained nothing, unless you were in a fixed account. But if you were two years away from retirement in 2008, with a nest egg of $700,000, and you sustained a loss of 30 percent, you would have lost $210,000. For most people, it took five years or more to regain the losses sustained in 2008—just to get their accounts back to even. That's five years of earning nothing. Put in that light, one year of earning nothing is pretty amazing.

Fixed index annuities can also provide tax-deferred growth of your funds, offering the potential for a strong return depending on indexed interest. Most importantly, a fixed index annuity guarantees both your principal and your gains if you follow all the guidelines carefully.

THE FINE PRINT

It's clear that fixed index annuities can have many upsides. If you match the right fixed index annuity with the right person, it can provide the ideal solution for retirement income generation. But it's also important that you approach any annuity with caution and seek the advice of a financial professional before purchasing one. There are a number of good reasons.

Be wary of surrender. Remember how not all annuities are created equal? This is one significant way they differ: surrender periods. Some insurance companies offer shorter surrender periods than others, and, if there's a chance you might need your money sooner rather than later, this is an important issue. If you find yourself in a bind and need your annuity premium back, you will pay a stiff penalty in many cases, losing up to 8-10 percent, depending on how long you've owned your annuity.

Promises, promises. Annuities can have confusing rates of return, and if you're buying one from someone who doesn't have a fiduciary duty to ensure that your best interests are protected, those rates of return could be misrepresented. In some cases, annuities can have hidden fees and charges as well. All of these are good reasons to work with a trusted financial professional to find the right annuity before making a purchase.

The right rider. Annuities come with a whole host of riders, many of which are covered below. Each of these riders comes with its own fee, and those fees vary from company to company. You should be sure that you're getting the right rider for your situation and not paying too much, which is a determination your financial professional can help you make. What's more, some people buy annuities with an income rider and *don't even know they have it.* They're paying an annual fee for a guaranteed income stream, and they don't even know to turn it on.

Tax Tip: As mentioned above, annuities come with surrender periods, which are specific lengths of time during which owners incur penalties if they decide to take their money out. Once the surrender period passes, owners have an option: they can execute a non-qualified tax-free exchange (1035 tax-free exchange), rolling the entire amount into a new annuity, which allows the whole balance to remain tax-deferred. One reason to do this would be to take advantage of a potentially higher interest rate, a bonus, or a new income rider. However, if the amount isn't rolled over into a new annuity, the annuity moves into the distribution phase—the phase during which the owner begins to receive income from the annuity.

INCOME RIDERS

An income rider is one of the potentially appealing options that annuities can deliver. For example, you might use $100,000 of your savings to buy a contract with an insurance company in the form of a fixed index annuity. That annuity could track with the S&P 500, the Dow Jones Industrial Average or any number of indexes. But you also decide to add something called an income rider, which is an attached benefit that guarantees a lifetime income stream, regardless of the premium balance of your annuity. Income riders can come with a variety of options, which can become confusing and complex. Here's a simplified breakdown. Your annuity has two columns: In one column, you have your premium, the amount you paid into that annuity. That's the amount you own and can withdraw (after your surrender period). An income rider starts a second column, in which money is invested to fund your guaranteed lifetime income stream. That money is guaranteed, but only in the sense that it will deliver a check to your door at the agreed-upon interval. Beyond that check, you can't access that sum of money, which can be confusing. It might seem like your $100,000 annuity has $250,000 of equity because of the balance in your income stream, but that's not the case. For some people, a guarantee income stream is the perfect option, but it's important to know what you're signing up for.

LONG-TERM CARE RIDERS

According to Morningstar, 40 percent of Americans who reach age 65 will need nursing home care in their lifetime, which can be a monumental cost, so long-term care is a very real possibility for everyone.* If your plan doesn't include a way to pay for long-term care, those costs will come out of your pocket, and that can mean a required spend-down of your assets before you

*http://news.morningstar.com/articlenet/article.aspx?id=564139

qualify for Medicaid. Rather than diminish the legacy you've been saving for your loved ones, one option for long-term healthcare planning is a long-term care rider. A long-term care rider (which can go by many names) allows you to use the annuity proceeds for long-term care.

Some people cover the long-term care needs with a long-term care policy, which is another option that has many benefits. However, in addition to being expensive, long-term care insurance also builds no equity: if you don't use it, you lose it. On the other hand, if you do not need your annuity's long-term care benefit, you still have the option of using your annuity's other benefits. For instance, you might also have an income rider attached to your annuity, or you could redeem your annuity at its maturity. Also, you can pass the remaining balance of your annuity to your loved ones as part of your legacy.

One consideration is that long-term care annuities often have the same qualification requirements as stand-alone long-term care insurance policies. You first have to be considered "insurable" by the annuity company, which means you have to answer questions relating to whether you have suffered any major illness such as cancer or heart disease, or whether you have a significant cognitive impairment like Alzheimer's disease. But you usually don't have to undergo a physical, and the underwriting is generally less stringent than with stand-alone long-term care insurance, meaning it's a little easier to qualify for the long-term care annuity.

Like most stand-alone long-term care policies, in order to be eligible for long-term care benefits from the annuity, you must be unable to accomplish at least two of six activities of daily living. They include feeding, bathing, dressing, transferring (moving about on your own), continence, and toileting. Thereafter, benefits are typically available after a waiting period of between 30 days and 2 years (depending on the particular product).

SINGLE PREMIUM IMMEDIATE ANNUITIES (SPIA)

A Single Premium Immediate Annuity is a contract between you and an insurance company in which you agree to give the insurance company a lump sum of money, and the insurance company agrees to give you a set payment at regular intervals. It's one way to replace that guaranteed monthly paycheck once you're no longer working. In some cases, a SPIA can provide peace of mind by delivering a guaranteed payment without worry about stock market volatility. But SPIAs are not the right fit for everyone, so before you commit any of your savings to one, it's important to take a careful look at what you're buying and what you're getting in return.

» *Lewis was 70 years old, and he had lost his patience with the stock market. He handles all of his own financial planning and stock portfolio, and for a while it was fun. He liked going online every day (or several times a day) to check his portfolio's performance, that is, until the stock market became so unpredictable. In the last ten years, Lewis's portfolio has been up and down so much, it has begun to make Lewis dizzy. Even worse, Lewis's portfolio never quite got back to its pre-2008 balance, and that made Lewis nervous. Lewis decided to take $100,000 from his portfolio, and he moved the remaining $150,000 to savings. With the $100,000, Lewis decided to purchase an SPIA, so that he would have some guaranteed income to count on. He already had a life insurance policy, so he bought his SPIA from the same company. That company agreed to begin sending him payments immediately of $416 each month. That amount would cover all of Lewis's utilities, and it took one worry off his mind.*

With that settled, Lewis decided to go skydiving, one of the last items on his bucket list. Sadly, Lewis had a heart attack *during his dive. He never used a dime of his $100,000 SPIA, and the insurance got to keep the full amount.*

Lewis's situation illustrates a few of the specific issues with SPIAs. One, once you make that lump sum payment, you have to be able to kiss it good-bye. With SPIAs, you retain no ownership of that principal. Also, Lewis only has $150,000 left from his stock portfolio after buying his SPIA. That's no small amount of money, but it will go quickly over the next 20 years. For people who aren't working with a large amount of savings, it can be a bad idea to tie a significant portion of savings up in an annuity of any kind. If you need access to your money in case of emergency, you don't want to tap out your entire savings. NOTE: One strategy we use with our clients where an SPIA may be a solid option for their need, is to tie a "period certain" clause into the payment structure. By doing this, either the client or their beneficiary will receive 100 percent of their asset back.

What's the bottom line? Always work with a trusted and independent financial professional before signing any contracts. Annuities are often sold by agents who receive healthy commissions. There's nothing wrong with receiving a commission, of course, but it does mean that the agent isn't committed to providing advice that's absolutely in your best interest. The most prudent choice is always get advice from someone on *your team* before making a financial decision that could affect your retirement lifestyle permanently.

Managing Risk Within Your Annuity:

Just like any investment strategy, the amount of risk needs to fit the comfort level of the investor. Annuities are no exception. Without going into too much detail, here are some additional ways to manage risk with annuity options:

If you want to structure an annuity investment for growth over a long period of time, you can select a variable annuity. The value of your principal investment follows the market and can lose or gain value with the market. This type of annuity can also have an income rider, but it is really more useful as an accumulation tool that bets on an improving market. A 40-year-old couple, for example, will probably want to structure more for growth and take on more risk than someone in their 70s. The 40-year-old couple may select a variable annuity with an income rider that kicks in when they plan to retire. If it rises with the market or outperforms it, the value of their investment has grown. If the market loses ground over the duration of the contract or their annuity underperforms, they can still rely on the income rider.

If you are 68 years old and you have more immediate income needs that you need to come up with above and beyond your Social Security, you need a low risk, reliable source of income. If you choose an annuity option, you are looking for something that will pay out an income right away over a relatively short timeframe. You probably want to opt for a SPIA that pays you immediately and spans a five year period, as well as an additional annuity that begins paying you in five years, and another longer term annuity that begins paying you in 10 years. Bear in mind that each annuity contract has its own costs and fees. Review these with your financial professional before you determine the best solutions and strategies for your situation.

The following example shows just how helpful an indexed annuity option can be for a retiree:

> » *Tanya is 60 years old and is wondering how she can use her assets to provide her with a retirement income. She has a $5,000 per month income need. If she starts withdrawing her Social Security benefit in six years at age 66, it will provide*

her with $2,200 per month. She also has a pension that kicks in at age 70 that will give her another $1,320 per month.

That leaves an income gap of $2,800 from ages 66 to 69, and then an income gap of $1,480 at age 70 and beyond. If Tanya uses only Green Money to solve her income need, she will need to deposit $918,360 at 2 percent interest to meet her monthly goal for her lifetime. If she opts to use Red Money and withdraws the amount she needs each month from the market, let's say the S & P 500, she will run out of cash in 10 years if she invested between the years of 2000 and 2012. Suffering a market downturn like that during the period for which she is relying on it for retirement income will change her life, and not for the better.

Working with a financial professional to find a better way, Tanya found that she could take a hybrid approach to fill her income gap. Her professional recommended two different income vehicles: one that allowed her to deposit just $190,161 with a 2 percent return, and one that was a $146,000 income annuity. These tools filled her income gap with $336,161, requiring her to spend $582,000 less money to accomplish her goal! Working with a professional to find the right tools for her retirement needs saved Tanya over half a million dollars.

CREATING AN INCOME PLAN

Creating an income plan before you retire allows you to satisfy your need for lifetime income and ensures that your lifestyle can last as long as you do. You also want to create a plan that operates in the most efficient way possible. Doing so will give more security to your Need Later Money and will potentially allow you to build your legacy down the road.

Here is a basic roadmap of what we have covered so far:

- Review your income needs and look specifically at the shortfall you may have during each year of your retirement based on your Social Security income, and income from any other assets you have.
- Ask yourself where you are in your distribution phase. Is retirement one year away? 10 years away? Last year?
- Determine how much money you need and how you need to structure your existing assets to provide for that need.
- If you have an asset from which you need to generate income, consider options offered by purchasing an income rider on an annuity.

» *Jeanne wants to retire at age 68. However, after her Social Security benefit, she will need nearly $375,000 in assets to generate a modest $40,000 of income per year.*

Amazingly, most people don't look ahead to think that at 68 years old, they will need $375,000 to have a basic lifestyle that pays out around $40,000 with Social Security benefits.

CHAPTER 5 RECAP //

- Having an income plan will help you get a picture of what your retirement is really going to look like.
- You have *Need Now Money* needs and *Need Later Money* needs. Creating an income plan is the first step toward providing for both of these needs.
- Maximizing your Social Security benefit depends on *when* and *how* you file.
- You'll need to examine your specific situation to find the best option for you.
- It's not impossible for you to calculate when the opportune time would be to trigger your Social Security income. In fact, with the tools and advice of a financial professional, it's quite easy.

- Integrating your Social Security options with the rest of your income plan will give you an idea of how much more money you need.
- Every dollar your Social Security income increases is less money you'll have to spend from your nest egg to supplement your income.
- After Social Security and your additional income are accounted for, the amount that's left to meet your needs is called the *Income Gap*.
- It is important to find ways to leverage your retirement assets to satisfy your need for lifetime income.
- It has been ages since many stocks returned meaningful dividends, so it isn't advisable to rely on them for reliable income. However, without stocks, your retirement plan will likely lose ground to inflation.
- It might be very attractive to have another asset, such as an annuity, that is designed to give you lifetime income. That income can go up in value as you wait to trigger a monthly check.
- If you think maximizing your Social Security isn't enough and you need the rest of your assets to be optimized to fill the income gap, an annuity may be a good option for you.
- Creating a retirement plan that focuses only on providing income will eventually have you cutting into your principle, drying it up in time and leaving you sucking up the last remaining drops.
- Although an annuity is an income-producing asset that does not subject your income to market risk, it still has the opportunity to grow.
- Be sure you understand the features, benefits, costs and fees associated with any annuity before you invest.

6

GROW YOUR FUTURE INCOME

"The broker is not your friend. He's more like a doctor who charges patients on how often they change medicines. And he gets paid far more for the stuff the house is promoting than the stuff that will make you better."

– Warren Buffet

Hire an Investment Advisory Firm
Using Social Security and a portion of your assets, you have secured a guaranteed income plan that will see you through retirement, no matter how long that retirement might last. Congratulations! Now it's time to think about the future. No one has a crystal ball, and if anyone claims to be able to predict the future, you probably shouldn't take any advice from that person. But there *are* a couple

of things we know about the future for sure: one, inflation happens and two, you will have to pay taxes.

Inflation: Inflation is one of the greatest risks to your well-being in retirement, but only if it isn't planned for properly. First, let's nail down the concept itself. Inflation is the increase in the cost of goods over time. If you remember buying a piece of gum for a penny when you were a kid, and you gasp at the $0.25 price tag on gum today, you're already familiar with inflation. Here's another: if you retired in the year 2000 and needed $5,000 per month to live on, in 2014 you would need $6,917.83 to pay for the exact same expenses.* That's quite a jump in just 14 years. What if you hadn't planned for that extra $1,917.83 that you needed?

For that reason, inflation is a very real worry for retirees. Fortunately, by working with a financial team that is focused on your best interests, you can plan for inflation by including a growth component in your retirement plan. After all, retirement should be full of fun, not anxiety.

Taxes: We'll discuss this more in Ch. 11, but an efficient retirement plan must always take into account the possibility that taxes will go up. This is another in the long line of very good reasons to have a financial team that covers all of the Big 4 on your side. By having a financial expert positioning your assets for growth, and a tax expert advising you on keeping your taxes as low as possible, you stand a much better chance of staying ahead of the Tax Man and keeping as much of your savings as possible.

Another thing that's likely to happen as you get older is that you will need more medical attention. As we discussed in Chapter 5, long-term healthcare of some kind is a common part of many retirements. According to one estimate, "more than two-thirds of 65-year-olds will need assistance to deal with a loss in functioning

---

*http://data.bls.gov/cgi-bin/cpicalc.pl

at some point during their remaining years of life."* If the required care includes a nursing home, those costs can be significant, to put it mildly. A U.S. News & World Report article summarized it like this: "In 2012, a private room cost an average of $248 daily, or more than $90,500 annually, according to a 2012 survey by MetLife. A semi-private room ran $222 daily, or more than $81,000 per year. And the average nursing home stay is 835 days, or more than two years, according to the government's latest National Nursing Home Survey."**

Long-term care options, such as long-term care insurance or a long-term care rider on an annuity or life insurance policy are some of the best options for planning for the costs of long-term care. But regardless of your long-term care needs, you still have those nagging issues of inflation and taxes, and that means another strategy that every retirement plan needs is growth.

By planning your strategy for guaranteed income carefully, the goal is to reserve some of your savings—your Need Later money—to be positioned for growth. Growth is necessary, but it can be a tricky thing thanks to the new volatility of our stock market.

MATH OF REBOUNDS

A fickle market can raise the eyebrows of even the most veteran investor. Taking a hit in the market hurts no matter how stable your income. Part of the pain comes from knowing that when you take a step back in the market, it requires an even larger step forward to return to where you were. As the market goes up and

---

*"Rising Demand for Long-term Services and Supports for Elderly People." Congressional Budget Office. June 2013. http://www.cbo.gov/publication/44363

**http://health.usnews.com/health-news/best-nursing-homes/articles/2013/02/26/how-to-pay-for-nursing-home-costs down, those larger gains you need to realize to get back to zero start to look even more daunting.

HOW REAL PEOPLE MAKE INVESTMENT DECISIONS

It can be challenging to watch the stock market's erratic changes every month, week or even every day. When you have your money riding on it, the ride can feel pretty bumpy. When you are managing your money by yourself, emotions inevitably enter into the mix. The Dow Jones Industrial Average and the S&P 500 represent more to you than market fluctuations. They represent a portion of your retirement. It's hard not to be emotional about it.

Everyone knows you should buy low and sell high. But this is what is more likely to happen:

The market takes a downturn, similar to the 2008 crash, and investors see as much as a 30 percent loss in their stock holdings. It's hard to watch, and it's harder to bear the pain of losing that much money. The math of rebounds means that they will need to rely on even larger gains just to get back to where things were before the downturn. They sell. But eventually, and inevitably, the market begins to rise again. Maybe slowly, maybe with some moderate growth, but by the time the average investor notices an upward trend and wants to buy in again, they have already missed a great deal of the gains.

CHAPTER 6 RECAP //

- No one can predict the future, but we do know that inflation and taxes will have a big effect on your retirement lifestyle if you don't plan for them properly.

- Long-term care is a cost that is likely to increase during your retirement years. Having a plan for accumulation can help meet that need.

- The Math of Rebounds shows that when you take a loss in the market, it requires an even greater gain just to get back to zero. That's just another factor that can create a frightening, emotional situation if you are handling your own investments.

7

AVOID EMOTIONAL INVESTING

"If you have more than $50,000 to invest, you should fire your broker and find an investment advisor. Brokerage firms would like you to think they perform the same functions as investment advisors."

– Arthur Levitt
Former Securities Exchange Commission Chairman

Beth is a proud investor in the home improvement company she has worked for these past 34 years. Not only did she receive numerous bonuses and pay raises during her tenure there, but also she received shares of stock in her company. The stock always did well, and everyone considered these stock bonuses to be a great incentive. In fact, Beth is such a believer in her company that she dedicates a significant portion of her paycheck to her monthly 401(k) contribution, earning the *maximum company match. Her 401(k) is also invested in company stock. As a result, Beth retires with $300,000 worth of company stock. That $300,000, however, constitutes the entirety of Beth's retirement. She loves her job and always planned to work until she was 70, but at age 62, she is diagnosed with rheumatoid arthritis and has to retire early. She isn't able to maximize her Social Security because of her health issues, and despite her conservative lifestyle, Beth still requires $3,500 each month to pay her bills. She begins selling $1,600 of her company stock each month to make ends meet. This seems like a good strategy, since she has $300,000 in stock, but $300,000 won't last her entire lifetime if it's reduced by $1,600 chunks every month. Fortunately for Beth, however, her sister insists that she consult her financial team. That meeting takes place in 2007, and Beth's team advises her to reposition her company holdings into a more diversified portfolio. Beth resists at first because loyalty is important to her. Finally, however, she realizes she has to take care of herself first.*

That was a very good decision. Just a few months later, Beth's company's stock took a major drop, along with much of the rest of the stock market. If Beth had kept her portfolio the same, she would have lost 20 percent of the value of her stock. In fact, she probably would have been forced to find a part time job. Instead, her financial professional restructured her portfolio at a much lower risk level, significantly reducing her losses. In just a couple of years, her investments were even and performing well.

In 2013, DALBAR, the well-respected financial services market research firm, released their annual "Quantitative Analysis of Investment Behavior" report (QAIB). The report studied the impact of market volatility on individual investors: people like Beth, or anyone who was managing (or mismanaging) their own investments in the stock market.

According to the study, volatility not only caused investors to make decisions based on their emotions, those decisions also harmed their investments and prevented them from realizing potential gains. So why do people meddle so much with their investments when the market is fluctuating? Part of the reason is that many people have financial obligations that they don't have control over. Significant expenses like house payments, the unexpected cost of replacing a broken-down car, and medical bills can put people in a position where they need money. If they need to sell investments to come up with that money, they don't have the luxury of selling when they *want* to. They must sell when they *need* to.

DALBAR's "Quantitative Analysis of Investor Behavior" has been used to measure the effects of investors' buying, selling and mutual fund switching decisions since 1994. The QAIB shows time and time again over nearly a 20-year period that the average investor earns less, and in many cases, significantly less than the performance of mutual funds suggests. QAIB's goal is to improve independent investor performance and to help financial professionals provide helpful advice and investment strategies that address the concerns and behaviors of the average investor.

An excerpt from the report claims that:*

"QAIB offers guidance on how and where investor behaviors can be improved. No matter what the state of the mutual fund industry, boom or bust: Investment results are more dependent on investor behavior than on fund performance. Mutual fund investors who hold on to their investments are more successful than those who time the market.

QAIB uses data from the Investment Company Institute (ICI), Standard & Poor's and Barclays Capital Index Products to compare mutual fund investor returns to an appropriate set of benchmarks.

---

*2013 QAIB, Dalbar, March 2013

There are actually three primary causes for the chronic shortfall for both equity and fixed income investors:
1. *Capital not available to invest. This accounts for 25 percent to 35 percent of the shortfall.*
2. *Capital needed for other purposes. This accounts for 35 percent to 45 percent of the shortfall.*
3. *Psychological factors. These account for 45 percent to 55 percent of the shortfall."*

The key findings of Dalbar's QAIB report provide compelling statistics about how individual investment strategies produced negative outcomes for the majority of investors:
- Psychological factors account for 45 percent to 55 percent of the chronic investment return shortfall for both equity and fixed income investors.
- Asset allocation is designed to handle the investment decision-making for the investor, which can materially reduce the shortfall due to psychological factors.
- Successful asset allocation investing requires investors to act on two critical imperatives:
  1. Balance capital preservation and appreciation so that they are aligned with the investor's objective.
  2. Select a qualified allocator.
- The best way for an investor to determine their risk tolerance is to utilize a risk tolerance assessment. However, these assessments must be accessible and usable.
- Evaluating allocator quality requires analysis of the allocator's underlying investments, decision making process and whether or not past efforts have produced successful outcomes.
- Choosing a top allocator makes a significant difference in the investment results one will achieve.

- Mutual fund retention rates suggest that the average investor has not remained invested for long enough periods to derive the potential benefits of the investment markets.
- Retention rates for asset allocation funds exceed those of equity and fixed income funds by over a year.
- Investors' ability to correctly time the market is highly dependent on the direction of the market. Investors generally guess right more often in up markets. However, in 2012 investors guessed right only 42 percent of the time during a bull market.
- Analysis of investor fund flows compared to market performance further supports the argument that investors are unsuccessful at timing the market. Market upswings rarely coincide with mutual fund inflows while market downturns do not coincide with mutual fund outflows.
- Average equity mutual fund investors gained 15.56 percent compared to a gain of 15.98 percent that just holding the S&P 500 produced.
- The shortfall in the long-term annualized return of the average mutual fund equity investor and the S&P 500 continued to decrease in 2012.
- The fixed-income investor experienced a return of 4.68 percent compared to an advance of 4.21 percent on the Barclays Aggregate Bond Index.
- The average fixed income investor has failed to keep up with inflation in nine out of the last 14 years.*

It doesn't take a financial services market research report to tell you that market volatility is out of your control. The report does prove, however, that before you experience market volatility, you should have an investment plan, and when the market is fluctuating, you

---

*2013 QAIB, Dalbar, March 2013

should stand by your investment plan. You should also review and discuss your investment plan with your financial professional on a regular basis, ensuring he/she is aware of any changes in your goals, financial circumstances, your health or your risk tolerance. When the economy is under stress and the markets are volatile, investors can feel vulnerable. That vulnerability causes people to tinker with their portfolios in an attempt to outsmart the market. Financial professionals, however, don't try to time the market for their clients. They try to tap into the gains that can be realized by committing to long-term investment strategies.

CHAPTER 7 RECAP //

- The DALBAR study demonstrated that the volatility of the stock market causes individual investors to react emotionally, and those investors tend to have less portfolio success overall.

- You cannot control the market, or predict it, but you can invest strategically. Consulting an investment advisor is a critical part of your strategic accumulation plan.

8

GROW WITH YELLOW MONEY

Once you've gotten a general idea of how your assets should be allocated after considering the Rule of 100, your risk tolerance, goals and objectives, and overall time horizon, you know how much Green Money you require to meet your immediate and mid-term income needs. You and your team now must decide the best strategy to create the growth you need to counter the inflation, tax and healthcare risks ahead of you in retirement. Growth often comes from investments in stocks, exchange traded funds, mutual funds and other investment solutions; however, unless those investments are managed with a specific purpose by a professional, they are Red Money. Under the watchful eye of a trusted investment advisor, however, that becomes Yellow Money and an engine for your retirement growth.

As you read earlier in the key findings of the DALBAR report, the deck is stacked against the individual investor. Remember that the average investor on a fixed income failed to keep pace with inflation in nine of the last 14 years, meaning the inherent risk in managing your Red Money is very real and could have a lasting impact on your assets. So, how much of your Red Money do you invest, and in what kinds of markets, investment solutions and stocks do you invest? There are a lot of different directions in which you can take your Red Money. One thing is for sure: significant accumulation depends on investing in the market. How you go about doing it is different for everyone. Gathering stocks, bonds and investment funds together in a portfolio without a cohesive strategy behind them could cause you to miss out on the benefits of a more thoughtful and planful approach. The end result is that you may never really understand what your money is doing, where and how it is really invested, and which investment principles are behind the investment solutions you hold. While you may have goals for each individual piece of your portfolio, it is likely that you don't have a comprehensive plan for your Red Money, which may mean that *you are taking on more risk than you would like, and are getting less return for it than is possible.*

Enter **Yellow Money.** Yellow Money is money that is managed by a professional *with a purpose.* After your income needs are met and you have assets that you would like to dedicate to accumulation, there are decisions you need to make about how to invest those assets. You can buy stocks, index funds, mutual funds, bonds — you name it — you can invest in it. However, the difference between Red Money and Yellow Money is that Yellow Money has a cohesive strategy behind it that is *implemented by a professional.* When you manage your Red Money with an investment plan, it becomes Yellow Money: *money that is being managed with a specific purpose, a specific set of focused goals and a specific strategy in mind.* Yellow Money is still a type of Red Money. It comes with different levels of risk. But Yellow Money is under the watchful eye of professionals who have a stake in the success of your money in the market and who can recommend a range of strategies from those designed for preservation to those targeting rapid growth. You don't want to miss out on achieving the right level of risk, and more importantly, composing a careful plan for the return of your assets.

While on a recent family trip to Europe, I thought of this analogy that may be helpful when thinking of red money and yellow money:

If you needed to travel through an unfamiliar city in a foreign country, you could rent a car or perhaps hire a driver. Were you to drive yourself, you would try to gain guidance from perplexing road signs and need to adhere to traffic rules—with no experience or assistance to lean on. It would take longer to get to where you want to go, and the chance of a traffic accident would be higher. If you hired a driver, they would manage your journey. A driver would know the route, how to avoid traffic, and follow the rules of the road.

Red Money is like driving yourself. With Yellow Money, you are still traveling by car, but now you have a professional working on your behalf.

TAKING A CLOSER LOOK AT YOUR PORTFOLIO

Think about your investment portfolio. Think specifically of what you would consider your Red Money. Do you know what is there? You may have several different investment solutions like individual mutual funds, bond accounts, stocks, etc. You may have inherited a stock portfolio from a relative, or you might be invested in a bond account offered by the company for which you worked due to your familiarity with them. While you may or may not be managing your investments individually, the reality is that you probably don't have an overall management strategy for all of your investments. Investments that aren't managed are simply Red Money, or money that is at risk in the market.

Harnessing the earning potential of your Red Money relies on more than a collection of stocks and bonds, however. It needs guided management. A good Yellow Money manager uses the knowledge they have about the level of risk with which you are comfortable, what you need or want to use your money for, when you want or need it and how you want to use it. The Yellow Money objects that they choose for you will still have a certain level of risk, but under the right management, control and process, you have a far better chance of a successful outcome that meets your specific needs.

When you sit down with an investment professional, you can look at all of your assets together. Chances are that you have accumulated a number of different assets over the last 20, 30 or 50 years. You may have a 401(k), an IRA, a Roth IRA, an account of self-directed stocks, a brokerage account, etc. Wherever you put your money, a financial professional will go through your assets and help you determine the level of risk to which you are exposed now and should be exposed in the future.

Here is a typical example of how an investment professional can be helpful to a future retiree with Yellow Money needs:

> » *Jane wants to retire in two years, and she has a 401(k) she has been contributing to for 26 years. In addition she has a stock portfolio, which was once managed by her late husband Harold. A few years ago, her sister told her about a hot mutual fund she read about in the paper and Jane, feeling like she should be doing more to prepare for retirement, invested $55,000 in that mutual fund as well as $30,000 in another mutual fund that she heard about on a TV news show.*
>
> *On her 65th birthday, Jane sits down with all of her financial papers. She looks at all of the statements and con-*

tracts covering her dining room table, and she feels a little dizzy. She realizes that she really has no idea what they mean for her retirement. She's been reacting to every story she reads or tip she hears, and now she has a whole bunch of assets that add up to what? She decides it's time to meet with an investment advisor.

At their first meeting, the advisor is ready with a whole set of questions:

1. Does she know exactly where all of her money is? *Jane doesn't know much about all her husband's stocks, which have now become hers. Their value is at $100,000 invested in three large cap companies. Jane is unsure of the companies and whether she should hold or sell them.*

2. Does she know what types of assets she owns? *Yes and no. She knows she has a 401(k), but she is unfamiliar with her husband's self-directed stock portfolio or the type of mutual funds she owns. Furthermore she is unclear as to how to manage the holdings as she nears retirement.*

3. Does she know the strategies behind each one of the investment solutions she owns? *While Jane knows she has a 401(k) and mutual fund holdings, she doesn't know how her 401(k) is organized or how to make it more conservative as she nears retirement. She really does not have specific investment principles guiding her investment decisions, and she doesn't know anything about her husband's individual stocks. One major concern for Jane is whether her family would be okay if she were not around?*

After determining Jane's assets, her financial professional prepares a consolidated report that lays out all of her assets for her to review. Her professional explains each one of them to her. Jane discovers that although she is two years away from retiring, her 401(k) is organized with an amount of risk with which she is not comfortable. Sixty percent of her 401(k) is at risk, far off the mark if we abide by the Rule of 100. Jane opts to be more conservative than the Rule of 100 suggests, as she will rely on her 401(k) for most of her immediate income needs after retirement. Jane's professional also points out several instances of overlap between her mutual funds. Jane learns that while she is comfortable with one of her mutual funds, she does not agree with the management principles of the other. In the end, Jane's professional helps her reorganize her 401(k) to secure her more Green Money for retirement income. Her professional also uses her mutual fund and her husband's stock assets to create a growth oriented investment plan that Jane will rely on for Need Later Money in 15 years when she plans on relocating closer to her children and grandchildren. By creating an overall investment strategy, Jane is able to meet her targeted goals in retirement. Jane's financial professional worked closely with her and her tax professional to minimize the tax impact of any asset sales on Jane's situation.

Like Jane, you may have several savings vehicles: a 401(k), an IRA to which you regularly contribute, some mutual funds to which you make monthly contributions, etc. But what is your *overall investment strategy?* Do you have one in place? Do you want one that will help you meet your retirement goals? Yellow Money managers look at *ALL* your accounts and all their different strategies to create a plan that helps them all work together. Your current investment situation may not reflect your wishes. As a matter of fact, it likely doesn't.

You may have a better understanding of your assets than Janet did, but even someone with an investment strategy can benefit from having a financial professional review their portfolio:

» *Charles is 69 years old. He retired four years ago. He relied on income from an IRA for three years in order to increase his Social Security benefit. He also made significant investments in 36 different mutual funds. He chose to diversify among the funds by selecting a portion for growth, another for good dividends, another that focused on promising small cap companies and a final portion that work like index funds. All the money that Charles had in mutual funds he considered Need Later Money that he wanted to rely on in his 80s. After the stock market took a hit in 2008, Charles lost some confidence in his investments and decided to sit down with a financial professional to see if his portfolio was able to recover.*

The professional Charles met with was able to determine what goals he had in mind. Specifically, the financial professional determined what Charles actually wanted and needed the money for, and when he needed it. His professional also looked inside each of the mutual funds and discovered several instances of overlap. While Charles had created diversity in his portfolio by selecting funds focused on different goals, he didn't account for overlap in the companies in which the funds were invested. Out of the 36 funds, his professional found that 20 owned nearly identical stock. While most of the companies were good investments, the high instance of overlap did not contribute to the healthy investment diversity that Charles wanted. Charles's financial professional also provided him with a report that explained the concentration ratio of his holdings (noting how much of his portfolio was contained within the top 25 stock holdings), the percentage of his portfolio that each company in which he invested in represented (showing the percentage of net assets that each company made up as an overall position in his portfolio) and the portfolio date of his account (showing when the funds in his portfolio were last updated: as funds are required to report updates only twice per year, it was possible that some of his fund reports could be six months old).

Charles's professional consolidated his assets into one investment management strategy. This allowed Charles's investments to be managed by someone he trusted who knew his specific investment goals and needs. Eliminating redundancy and overlap in his portfolio was easy to do but difficult to detect since Charles had multiple funds with multiple brokerage firms. Charles sat down with a professional to see if his mutual funds could perform well, and he left with a consolidated management plan and a money manager that understood him personally. That's Yellow Money at its best.

AVOIDING EMOTIONAL INVESTING

There's no way around it; people get emotional about their money. And for good reason. You've spent your life working for it, exchanging your time and talent for it, and making decisions about how to invest it, save it and make it grow. The maintenance of your lifestyle and your plans for retirement all depend on it. The best investment strategies, however, don't rely on emotions. One of Yellow Money's greatest strengths lies in the fact that it is managed by someone who understands your needs and desires, but doesn't make decisions about your money under the influence of emotion.

A well-managed investment account meets your goals as a whole, not in individualized and piecemeal ways. Professional money managers do this by creating requirements for each type of investment in which they put your money. We'll call them "screens." Your money manager will run your holdings through the screens they have created to evaluate different types of investment strategies. A professionally managed account will only have holdings that meet the requirements laid out in the overall management plan that was designed to meet your investment goals. The holdings that don't make it through the screens, the ones that don't contribute to your investment goals, are sold and redistributed to investments that your financial professional has determined to be appropriate.

Different screens apply to different Yellow Money strategies. For example, if one of your goals is significant growth, which would require taking on more risk alongside the potential for more return, an investment professional would screen for companies that have high rates of revenue and sales growth, high earnings growth, rising profit margins, and innovative products. On the other hand, if you want your portfolio to be used for income, which would call for lower risk and less return, your professional would screen for dividend yield and sector diversification. *Every investor has a different goal, and every goal requires a customized strategy that uses quantitative screens.* A professional will create a portfolio that reflects your investment desires. If some of the current assets you own complement the strategies that your professional recommends, those will likely stay in your portfolio.

Screening your assets removes emotions from the equation. It removes attachment to underperforming or overly risky investments. Financial professionals aren't married to particular stocks or mutual funds for any reason. They go by the numbers and see your portfolio through a lens shaped by your retirement goals. Your professional understands your wants and needs, and creates an investment strategy that takes your life events and future plans into account. It's a planful approach, and it allows you to tap into the tools and resources of a professional who has built a career around successful investing. Managing money is a full-time job and is best left to a professional money manager.

Removing emotions from investing also allows you to be unaffected by the day-to-day volatility of the market. Your financial professional doesn't ask where the market is going to be in a year, three years or a month from now. If you look at the value of the

stock market from the beginning of the twentieth century to today, it's going up. Despite the Great Depression, despite the 1987
crash, despite the 2008 market downturn, the market, as a whole,
trends up. Remember the major market downturn in 2008 when
the market lost 30 percent of its value? Not only did it completely
recover, it has far exceeded its 2008 value. Emotional investing
led countless people to sell low as the market went down, and buy
the same shares back when the market started to recover. That's
an expensive way to do business. While you can't afford to lose
money that you need in two, three or five years, your Need Later
Money has time to grow. The best way to do so is to make it
Yellow.

CREATING AN INVESTMENT STRATEGY

Just like Jane and Charles, chances are that you can benefit from
taking a more managed investment approach tailored to your
goals. Yellow Money is generally Need Later Money that you
want to grow for needs you'll have in at least 10 years. You can
work with your financial planner to create investments that meet
your needs within different timeframes. You may need to rely on
some of your Yellow Money in 10, 15 or 20 years, whether for
additional income, a large purchase you plan on making or a vacation. Whatever you want it for, you will need it down the road. A
financial professional can help you rescale the risk of your assets
as they grow, helping you lock in your profits and secure a source
of income you can depend on later.

So what does a Yellow Money account look like? Here's what
it *doesn't* look like: a portfolio with 49 small cap mutual funds,
a dozen individual stocks and an assortment of bond accounts.
A brokerage account with a hodgepodge of investments, even if
goal-oriented, is not a professionally managed account. It's still
Red Money. Remember, Yellow Money is a managed account that
has an overarching investment philosophy. When you look at

making investments that will perform to meet your future income needs, the burning question becomes: How much should you have in the market and how should it be invested? Working with a professional will help you determine how much risk you should take, how to balance your assets so they will meet your goals and how to plan for the big ticket items, like health care expenses, that may be in your future. Yes, Yellow Money is exposed to risk, but by working with a professional, you can manage that risk in a productive way.

WHY YELLOW MONEY?

If you have met your immediate income needs for retirement, why bother with professionally managing your other assets? The money you have accumulated above and beyond your income needs probably has a greater purpose. It may be for your children or grandchildren. You may want to give money to a charity or organization that you admire. In short, you may want to craft your legacy. It would be advantageous to grow your assets in the best manner possible. A financial professional has built a career around managing money in profitable ways. They are experts under the supervision of the organization that they represent.

Turning to Yellow Money also means that you don't have to burden yourself with the time commitment, the stress, and the cost of determining how to manage your money. Yellow Money can help you better enjoy your retirement. Do you want to sit down in your home office every day and determine how to best allocate your assets, or do you want to be living your life while someone else manages your money for you? When the majority of your Red Money is managed with a specific purpose by a financial professional, you don't have to be worrying about which stocks to buy and sell today or tomorrow.

SEEKING FINANCIAL ADVICE: STOCK BROKERS VS. INVESTMENT ADVISOR REPRESENTATIVES

Investors basically have access to two types of advice in today's financial world: advice from stock brokers and advice given by investment advisors. Most investors, however, don't know the difference between types of advice and the people from whom they receive advice. Today, there are two primary types of advice offered to investors: advice given by a commission-based registered representative (brokers) and advice given by fee-based Investment Advisor Representatives. Unfortunately, many investors are not aware that a difference exists; nor have they been explained the distinction between the two types of advice. In a survey taken by TD Ameritrade, the top reasons investors choose to work with an independent registered investment advisor are:*

- Registered Investment Advisors are required, as fiduciaries, to offer advice that is in the best interest of clients
- More personalized service and competitive fee structure offered at a Registered Investment Advisor firm
- Dissatisfaction with full commission brokers

The truth is that there is a great deal of difference between stock brokers and investment advisor representatives. For starters, investment advisor representatives are obligated to act in an investor's best interests in all aspects of a financial relationship. Confusion continues to exist among investors struggling to find the best financial advice out there and the most credible sources of advice.

Here is some information to help clear up the confusion so you can find good advice from a professional you can trust:

---

*2011 Advisor Sentiment Study, commissioned by TD AMERITRADE. TD Ameritrade, Inc.

- Investment advisor representatives have the fiduciary duty to act in a client's best interest at all times with every investment decision they make. Stock brokers and brokerage firms usually do not act as fiduciaries to their investors and are not obligated to make decisions that are entirely in the best interest of their customers. For example, if you decide you want to invest in precious metals, a stock broker would offer you a precious metals account from their firm. An Investment Advisor would find you a precious metals account that is the best fit for you based on the investment strategy of your portfolio.
- Investment advisors give their clients a Form ADV describing the methods that the professional uses to do business. An Investment Advisor also obtains client consent regarding any conflicts of interest that could exist with the business of the professional.
- Stock brokers and brokerage firms are not obligated to provide comparable types of disclosure to their customers.
- Whereas stock brokers and firms routinely earn large profits by trading as principal with customers, Investment Advisors cannot trade with clients as principal (except in very limited and specific circumstances).
- Investment Advisors charge a pre-negotiated fee with their clients in advance of any transactions. They cannot earn additional profits or commissions from their customers' investments without prior consent. Registered Investment Advisors are commonly paid an asset-based fee that aligns their interests with those of their clients. Brokerage firms and stock brokers, on the other hand, have much different payment agreements. Their revenues may increase regardless of the performance of their customers' assets.
- Unlike brokerage firms, where investment banking and underwriting are commonplace, Registered Investment

Advisors must manage money in the best interests of their customers. Because Registered Investment Advisors charge set fees for their services, their focus is on their client. Brokerage firms may focus on other aspects of the firm that do not contribute to the improvement of their clients' assets.

- Unlike brokers, Registered Investment Advisors typically do not get commissions from fund or insurance companies for providing their investment solutions.

Just to drive home the point, here is what a fiduciary duty to a client means for a Registered Investment Advisor. Registered Investment Advisors must:*

- Always act in the best interest of their client and make investment decisions that reflect their goals.
- Identify and monitor securities that are illiquid.
- When appropriate, employ fair market valuation procedures.
- Observe procedures regarding the allocation of investment opportunities, including new issues and the aggregation of orders.
- Have policies regarding affiliated broker-dealers and maintenance of brokerage accounts.
- Disclose all conflicts of interest.
- Have policies on use of brokerage commissions for research.
- Have policies regarding directed brokerage, including step-out trades and payment for order flow.
- Abide by a code of ethics.

2011 Advisor Sentiment Study, commissioned by TD AMERITRADE. TD Ameritrade, Inc.

CHAPTER 8 RECAP //

- Yellow Money may make Red Money less dangerous.
- Yellow Money is professionally managed.
- Yellow Money has a cohesive purpose and a strategy behind it.
- If you haven't sat down and thought about how much money you need in order to generate income during retirement, you're just speculating.
- Red Money is like driving yourself in unfamiliar territory. With Yellow Money, you are still traveling by car, but now you have a professional driving on your behalf.
- The deck is stacked against the ordinary investor. According to the DALBAR report, individual investors consistently underperform compared to the market because of a variety of factors, including emotional investing.
- Yellow Money is managed without emotions.
- Checking your truly Red Money should be like checking the sports section. You are interested in it, but it won't directly affect your lifestyle. If your Red Money goes down 50 percent, no one should have to scrape you off the floor.

9

USE NEW WORLD INVESTING IDEAS

In Chapter 1, we discussed how today's investment options require advice that is relevant to today. Traditional, outdated investment strategies are not only ineffective, they can be harmful to the average investor. One of the most traditional ways of thinking about investing is the risk versus reward trade-off. It goes something like this.

Investment options that are considered safer carry less risk, but also offer the potential for less return. Riskier investment options carry the burden of volatility and a greater potential for loss, but they also offer a greater potential for large rewards. Most professionals move their clients back and forth along this range, shifting between investments that are safer and investments that are structured for growth. Essentially, the old rules of investing dictate that you can either choose relative safety *or* return, but you can't have both.

Updated investment strategies work with the flexibility of liquidity to remake the rules. Here is how:

There are three dimensions that are inherent in any investment: *Liquidity, Safety,* and *Return.* You can maximize any two of these dimensions at the expense of the third. If you choose Safety and Liquidity, this is like keeping your assets in a checking account or savings account. This option delivers a lot of Safety and Liquidity, but at the expense of any Return. On the other hand, if you choose Liquidity and Return, meaning you have the potential for great return and can still reclaim your money whenever you choose, you will likely be exposed to a very high level of risk.

Understanding Liquidity can help you break the old Risk versus Safety trade-off. By identifying assets from which you don't require Liquidity, you can place yourself in a position to potentially profit from relatively safe investments that provide a higher than average rate of return.

Choosing Safety and Return over Liquidity can have significant impacts on the accumulation of your assets. In Ted's case, the paradigm shift from earning and saving to leveraging assets was a costly one.

» *Ted is a corn and soybean farmer with 1,200 acres of land. He routinely retains somewhere between $40,000 and $80,000 in his checking and savings accounts. If a major piece of equipment fails and needs repair or replacement, Ted will need the money available to pay for the equipment and carry on with farming. If the price of feed for his cattle goes up one year, he will need to compensate for the increased overhead to his farming operation. He isn't a particularly wealthy farmer, but he has little choice but to keep a portion of money on hand in case something comes up and he must* *access it quickly. Most of his capital is held in livestock in the pasture or crops in the ground tied up for six to eight months of the year. When a major financial need arises, Ted can't just harvest 10 acres of soybeans and use them for payment. He needs to depend heavily on Liquidity in order to be a successful farmer.*

Old habits die hard, however, and when Ted finally hangs up his overalls and quits farming, he keeps his bank accounts flush with cash, just like in the old days. After selling the farm and the equipment, Ted keeps a huge portion of the profits in Liquid investments because that's what he is familiar with. Unfortunately for Ted, with his pile of money sitting in his checking account, he isn't even keeping pace with inflation. After all his hard work as a farmer, his money is losing value every day because he didn't shift to a paradigm of leveraging his assets to generate income and accumulate value.

Almost anything would be a better option for Ted than clinging to Liquidity. He could have done something better to get either more return from his money or more safety, and at the very least would not have lost out to inflation.

As you can see, choosing Liquidity solely can be a costly option. The sooner you want your money back, the less you can leverage it for Safety or Return. If you have the option of putting your money in a long-term investment, you will be sacrificing Liquidity, but potentially gaining both Safety and Return. Rethinking your approach to money in this way can make a world of difference and can provide you with a structured way to generate income while allowing the value of your asset to grow over time.

The question is, how much Liquidity do you *really* need? Think about it. If you haven't sat down and created an income plan for your retirement, your perceived need for Liquidity is a guess. You don't know how much cash you'll need to fill the income gap if you don't know the amount of your Social Security benefit or the total of your other income options. If you *have* determined your income need and have made a plan for filling your income gap, you can partition your assets based on when you will need them. With an income plan in place, ***you can use new rules to enjoy both Safety and Return from your assets.***

CHAPTER 9 RECAP //

- There are three dimensions that are inherent in any investment: *Liquidity, Safety,* and *Return.* You can maximize any two of these dimensions at the expense of the third.
- Understanding Liquidity can help you break the old Risk versus Safety trade-off.

10

LIMIT THE IMPACT
OF TAXES

*Stephen and Malita have saved diligently, and their years of dedica-
tion have resulted in a large retirement account: $3 million. They're
both just approaching 60, but they're not planning on retiring for
a few years. They are concerned, however about the positioning of
their assets. In addition to Malita's pension, they have $2 million in
an IRA, which is exposed to market risk. In addition, their IRA is
a traditional one. They haven't paid any taxes on those savings, and
they're concerned about how that will impact them in retirement.
They went to visit with their financial team to ask what they could do
to limit their tax liability.*

*That's a question every retiree should ask. The answer, for Stephen
and Malita is a Roth IRA conversion, but the KEY to that conversion
is to do it bit by bit. If they withdrew their entire IRA at once and*

rolled it into a Roth, can you imagine what their tax bracket would be that year? It's painful even to consider! However, if that transition is orchestrated slowly over the next 15 years, making smaller withdrawals, their tax liability is limited, allowing them to keep more of their savings.

Taxes play a starring role in the theater of retirement planning. Everyone is familiar with taxes (you've been paying them your entire working life), but not everyone is familiar with how to make tax planning a part of their retirement strategy.

Taxes are taxes, right? You'll pay them before retirement and you'll pay them during retirement. What's the difference? The truth is that a planful approach to taxes can help you save money, protect your assets and ensure that your legacy remains intact. And the easiest way to create a planful approach that optimizes every part of your retirement plan is to work with a financial team that communicates with you and the overall professional team, and coordinates your retirement every step of the way.

How can a tax form do all that? The answer lies in planning. **Tax planning** and **tax reporting** are two very different things. Most people only *report* their taxes. March rolls around, people pull out their 1040s or use TurboTax to enter their income and taxable assets, and ship it off to Uncle Sam at the IRS. If you use a CPA to report your taxes, you are essentially paying them to record history. You have the option of being proactive with your taxes and to plan for your future by making smart, informed decisions about how taxes affect your overall financial plan. Working with a financial professional who, along with a CPA, makes recommendations about your finances to you, will keep you looking forward instead of in the rearview mirror as you enter retirement. It is much better to be proactive versus reactive.

TAXES AND RETIREMENT

When you retire, you move from the earning and accumulation phase of your life into the asset distribution phase of your life. For most people, that means relying on Social Security, a 401(k), an IRA, or a pension. Wherever you have put your Green Money for retirement, you are going to start relying on it to provide you with the income that once came as a paycheck. Most of these distributions will be considered income by the IRS and will be taxed as such. There are exceptions to that (not all of your Social Security income is taxed, and income from Roth IRAs is not taxed), but for the most part, your distributions will be subject to income taxes.

Regarding assets that you have in an IRA or a 401(k) plan that uses an IRA, when you reach 70 ½ years of age, you will be required to draw a certain amount of money from your IRA as income each year. That amount depends on your age and the balance in your IRA. The amount that you are required to withdraw as income is called a Required Minimum Distribution (RMD). Why are you required to withdraw money from your own account? Chances are the money in that account has grown over time, and the government wants to collect taxes on that growth. If you have a large balance in an IRA, there's a chance your RMD could increase your income significantly enough to put you into a higher tax bracket, subjecting you to a higher tax rate.

Here's where tax planning can really begin to work strongly in your favor. In the distribution phase of your life, you have a predictable income based on your RMDs, your Social Security benefit and any other income-generating assets you may have. What really impacts you at this stage is how much of that money you keep in your pocket after taxes. Essentially, *you will make more money saving on taxes than you will by making more money.* If you can reduce your tax burden by 30, 20 or even 10 percent, you earn yourself that much more money by not paying it in taxes.

How do you save money on taxes? By having a plan. In this instance, a financial professional can work with the CPAs at their firm to create a **distribution plan** that minimizes your taxes and maximizes your annual net income.

BUILDING A TAX DIVERSIFIED PORTFOLIO

So far so good: avoid taxes, maximize your net annual income and have a plan for doing it. When people decide to leverage the experience and resources of a financial professional, they may not be thinking of how distribution planning and tax planning will benefit their portfolios. Often more exciting prospects like planning income annuities, investing in the market and structuring investments for growth rule the day. Taxes, however, play a crucial role in retirement planning. Achieving those tax goals requires knowledge of options, foresight and professional guidance.

Finding the path to a good tax plan isn't always a simple task. Every tax return you file is different from the one before it because things constantly change. Your expenses change. Planned or unplanned purchases occur. Health care costs, medical bills, an inheritance, property purchases, reaching an age where your RMD kicks in or travel, any number of things can affect how much income you report and how many deductions you take each year.

Preparing for the ever-changing landscape of your financial life requires a tax-diversified portfolio that can be leveraged to balance the incomes, expenditures and deductions that affect you each year. A financial professional will work with you to answer questions like these:

- What does your tax landscape look like?
- Do you have a tax-diversified portfolio robust enough to adapt to your needs?

- Do you have a diversity of taxable and non-taxable income planned for your retirement?
- Will you be able to maximize your distributions to take advantage of your deductions when you retire?
- Is your portfolio strong enough and tax-diversified enough to adapt to an ever-changing (and usually increasing) tax code?

» *When Darlene returns home after a week in the hospital recovering from a knee replacement, the 77-year-old calls her daughter, sister and brother to let them know she is home and feeling well. She also should have called her CPA. Darlene's medical expenses for the procedure, her hospital stay, her medications and the ongoing physical therapy she attended amount to more than $50,000.*

Currently, Americans can deduct medical expenses that are more than 7.5 percent of their Adjusted Gross Income (AGI). Darlene's AGI is $60,000 the year of her knee replacement, meaning she is able to deduct $44,000 of her medical bills from her taxes that year. Her AGI dictated that she could deduct more than 80 percent of her medical expenses that year. **Darlene didn't know this.**

Had she been working with a financial professional who regularly asked her about any changes in her life, her spending, or her expenses (expected or unexpected), Darlene could have saved thousands of dollars. Darlene can also file an amendment to her tax return to recoup the overpayment.

This relatively simple example of how tax planning can save you money is just the tip of the iceberg. No one can be expected to know the entire U.S. tax code. But a professional who is working with a team of CPAs and financial professionals has an advantage over the average taxpayer who must start from square one on their own every year. Have you been taking advantage of all the deductions that are available to you?

PROACTIVE TAX PLANNING

The implications of proactive tax planning are far reaching, and are larger than many people realize. Remember, doing your taxes in January, February, March or April means you are writing a history book. Planning your taxes in October, November or December means that you are writing the story as it happens. You can look at all the factors that are at play and make decisions that will impact your tax return *before* you file it.

Realizing that tax planning is an aspect of financial planning is an important leap to make. When you incorporate tax planning into your financial planning strategy, it becomes part of the way you maximize your financial potential. Paying less in taxes means you keep more of your money. Simply put, the more money you keep, the more of it you can leverage as an asset. This kind of planning can affect you at any stage of your life. If you are 40 years old, are you contributing the maximum amount to your 401(k) plan? Are you contributing to a Roth IRA? Are you finding ways to structure the savings you are dedicating to your children's education? Do you have life insurance? Taxes and tax planning affects all of these investment tools. Having a relationship with a professional who works with a CPA can help you build a truly comprehensive financial plan that not only works with your investments, but also shapes your assets to find the most efficient ways to prepare for tax time. There may be years that you could benefit from higher distributions because of the tax bracket that you are in, or there could be years you would benefit from taking less. There may be years when you have a lot of deductions and years you have relatively few. **Adapting your distributions to work in concert with your available deductions** is at the heart of smart tax planning. Professional guidance can bring you to the next level of income distribution, allowing you to remain flexible enough to maximize your tax efficiency. And remember, saving money on taxes makes you more money than making money does.

What you have on paper is important: your assets, savings, investments, which are a financial expression of your work and time. It's just as important to know how to get it off the paper in a way that keeps most of it in your pocket. Almost anything that involves financial planning also involves taxes. Annuities, investments, IRAs, 401(k)s, 403(b), and many other investment options will have tax implications. Life also has a way of throwing curveballs. Illness, expensive car repair or replacement, or *any event that has a financial impact on your life will likely have a corresponding tax implication* around which you should adapt your financial plan. Tax planning does just that.

One dollar can end up being less than 25 cents to your heirs.

» *When Peter's father passed away, he discovered that he was the beneficiary of his father's $500,000 IRA. Peter has a wife and a family of four children, and he knew that his father had intended for a large portion of the IRA to go toward funding their college educations.*

After Peter's father's estate is distributed, Peter, who is 50 years old and whose two oldest sons are entering college, liquidates the IRA. By doing so, his taxable income for that year puts him in a 39.6 percent tax bracket, immediately reducing the value of the asset to $302,000. An additional 3.8 percent surtax on net investment income further diminishes the funds to $283,000. Liquidating the IRA in effect subjects much of Peter's regular income to the surtax, as well. At this point, Peter will be taxed at 43.4 percent.

Peter's state taxes are an additional 9 percent. Moreover, estate taxes on Peter's father's assets claim another 22 percent.

By the time the IRS is through, Peter's income from the IRA will be taxed at 75 percent, leaving him with $125,000 of the original $500,000. While it would help contribute to the education of his children, it wouldn't come anywhere near completely paying for it, something the $500,000 could have easily done.

As the above example makes clear, leaving an asset to your beneficiaries can be more complicated than it may seem. In the case of a traditional IRA, after federal, estate and state taxes, the asset could literally diminish to as little as 25 percent of its value.

How does working with a professional help you make smarter tax decisions with your own finances? Any financial professional worth their salt will be working with a firm that has a team of trained tax professionals, including CPAs, who have an intimate knowledge of the tax code and how to adapt a financial plan to it.

Here's another example of how taxes have major implications on asset management:

» *Greg and Rhonda, a 62-year-old couple, begin working with a financial professional in October. After structuring their assets to reflect their risk tolerance and creating assets that would provide them Green Money income during retirement, they feel good about their situation. They make decisions that allow them to maximize their Social Security benefits, they have plenty of options for filling their income gap, and have begun a safe yet ambitious Yellow Money strategy with their professional. When their professional asks them about their tax plan, they tell him their CPA handled their taxes every year, and did a great job. Their professional says, "I don't mean who does your taxes, I mean, who does your tax planning?" Greg and Rhonda aren't sure how to respond.*

Their professional brings Greg and Rhonda's financial plan to the firm's CPA and has her run a tax projection for them. A week later their professional calls them with a tax plan for the year that will save them more than $3,000 on their tax return. The couple is shocked. A simple piece of advice from the CPA based on the numbers revealed that if they paid their estimated taxes before the end of the year, they would be able to itemize it as a deduction, allowing them to save thousands of dollars.

This solution won't work for everyone, and it may not work for Greg and Rhonda every year. That's not the point. By being proactive with their approach to taxes and using the resources made available by their financial professional, they were able to create a tax plan that saved them money.

YELLOW MONEY AND TAXES

There are also tax implications for the money that you have managed professionally. People with portions of their investment portfolio that are actively traded can particularly benefit from having a proactive tax strategy. Without going into too much detail, for tax purposes there are two kinds of investment money: qualified and non-qualified. Different investment strategies can have different effects on how you are taxed on your investments and the growth of your investments. Some are more beneficial for one kind of investment strategy over another. Determining how to plan for the taxation of non-qualified and qualified investments is fodder for holiday party discussions at accounting firms. While it may not be a stimulating topic for the average investor, you don't have to understand exactly how it works in order to benefit from it.

While there are many differences between qualified and non-qualified investments, the main difference is this: qualified plans are designed to give investors tax benefits by deferring taxation of their growth until they are withdrawn. Non-qualified investments are not eligible for these deferral benefits. As such, non-qualified investments are taxed whenever income is realized from them in the form of growth.

Actively and non-actively traded investments provide a simple example of how to position your investments for the best tax advantage. In an actively traded and managed portfolio, there is a high amount of buying and selling of stocks, bonds, mutual funds, ETFs, etc. If that active portfolio of non-qualified investments does well and makes a 20 percent return one year and you are in the 39.6 percent tax bracket, your net gain from that portfolio is only about 12 percent (39.6 percent tax of the 20 percent gain is roughly 8 percent.) In a passive trading strategy, you can use a qualified investment tool, such as an IRA, to achieve 13, 14 or 15 percent growth (much lower than the actively traded portfolio), but still realize a higher net return because the growth of the qualified investment is not taxed until it is withdrawn.

Does this mean that you have to always rely on a buy and hold strategy in qualified investment tools? Not necessarily. The question is, if you have qualified and non-qualified investments, where do you want to position your actively traded and managed assets? Incorporating a planful approach to positioning your investments for more beneficial taxation can be done many ways, but let's consider one example. Keeping your actively managed investment strategies inside an IRA or some other qualified plan could allow you to realize the higher gains of those investments without paying tax on their growth every year. Your more passively managed funds could then be kept in taxable, non-qualified vehicles and methods, and because you aren't realizing income from them on an annual basis by frequently trading them, they grow sheltered from taxation.

If you are interested in taking advantage of tax strategies that maximize your net income, you need the attentive strategies, experience and knowledge of a professional who can give you options that position you for profit. At the end of the day, what's important to you as the consumer is how much you keep, your after-tax take home.

ESTATE TAXES

The government doesn't just tax your income from investments while you're alive. They will also dip into your legacy.

While estate taxes aren't as hot of a topic as they were a few years ago, they are still an issue of concern for many people with assets. While taxes may not apply on estates that are less than $5 million, certain states have estate taxes with much lower exclusion ratios. Some are as low as $600,000. Many people may have to pay a state estate tax. One strategy for avoiding those types of taxes is to move assets outside of your estate. That can include gifting them to family or friends, or putting them into an irrevocable trust. Life insurance is another option for protecting your legacy.

CHAPTER 10 RECAP //

- A tax-diversified portfolio that can be leveraged to balance your income, expenditures and deductions to your greatest advantage.
- When you incorporate tax planning into your financial planning strategy, it becomes part of the way you maximize your financial potential.

11

UNDERSTAND THE FUTURE OF TAXES

Tax legislation over the course of American history has left one very resounding message: taxes go up. Sadly, we hear this same threat so often that it has begun to sound like the boy who cried wolf. The reason behind this lies in the fact that tax hikes usually do not take effect until two or three years after their introduction and subsequently get piecemeal implementation. The result of this prolonged implementation period can be equated to death by a thousand paper cuts.

DEBT CEILING – CAUSE AND EFFECTS

The raising of the debt ceiling raised more than just the ability for our government to go further into debt. It also raised concerns and fears about the future of our economy. We are now seeing major swings in the markets with investors showing serious concerns over the future of investment valuations and their personal wealth. Unfortunately, the reasoning behind all of this uncertainty is preceded by the inability to see the full implications of what is in store. We rarely talk about the fact that the discussions on raising the debt ceiling were coupled to discussions on major tax reforms needed to correct the problems underlining the debt ceiling increase itself.

Increasing the debt ceiling was needed because the government maxed out its credit card, so to speak, which it has been living off of for quite some time. It is really not much different than what we have been seeing from the general public for the past few decades. Unfortunately, most of us do not have the ability to get a credit limit increase on our credit cards once we reach the maximum limit; that is, unless we can show the ability to pay this balance back. The only way to pay this credit card back is by spending less and making more money.

This is exactly where the federal government is today. They have been given a higher credit limit, but they still must find a way to decrease the spending while making more money. The only way the government makes money is by collecting taxes.

Unfortunately, at the current moment, the government is collecting approximately $120 billion less per month than it currently spends. Discussions for major tax reform have accompanied the discussions for the increased debt ceiling.

DEBT AND EARNINGS

Let us take a closer look at where we are today. The U.S. national debt is increasing at an alarming rate, rising to levels never seen before and threatening serious harm to the economy. Through the end of 2010, the national debt has risen to $13.6 trillion, averaging an 11.4 percent increase annually over the past five years and a 9.2 percent increase annually over the past 10 years. To put this into perspective, the national gross domestic product (GDP) has increased to $14.5 trillion during the same period, averaging a 2.9 percent annual increase over the past five years and a 3.9 percent increase over the past 10 years. At the end of 2010, the national debt level was 93 percent of the GDP. Economists believe that a sustainable economy exists at a maximum level of approximately 80 percent. As of December 20, 2013, the U.S. national debt is 107.69 percent of GDP with the debt at $17.252 trillion and the GDP at $16.020 trillion.*

The significance of these two numbers lies within the contrast. The national debt is the amount that needs to be repaid. This is the credit card balance. Gross domestic product on the other hand is less known and represents the market value of all final goods and services produced within a country during a given period. Essentially, GDP represents the gross taxable income available to the government. If debts are increasing at a greater rate than the gross income available for taxation, then the only way to make up the difference is by increasing the rate at which the gross income is taxed.

The most recent presidential budget shows a continuing trend in the disparity between growth in the national debt and GDP over the next two decades. Although the increasing disparity is a real concern and shows that, at least in the short run, the federal deficit will not be addressed to counteract the potential crisis ahead, it is the revenue collection that tells the disconcerting story. Over the past 40 years the average collection of GDP has been approximately 17.6 percent and currently collections are at approximately 14.4 percent of GDP.

As the presidential budget reveals, the projected revenues are estimated to be 20 percent by the end of the next decade. That is a 38.8 percent increase from the current tax levels. To put this

---

http://www.usdebtclock.org/12/20/13

into perspective, if you are currently in the top tax bracket of 35 percent and this bracket increases by the proposed collection increase, your tax rate will be approximately 48.5 percent. Keep in mind that even at this rate the deficit is projected to increase.

2013 – THE END OF AN ERA?

From a historical point of view, taxes are extremely low. The last time the U.S. national debt was at the same percentage level of GDP as today was at the end of World War II and several years following. The maximum tax rate averaged 90 percent from 1944 through 1963. Compare that to the maximum rate of 35 percent today and it becomes very clear that there is a disparity of extreme proportion.

Taxes during this historical period were at extreme levels for nearly 20 years, during and following this current level of debt-to-GDP. A significant point to note about the difference between that time and today is the economic activity. The period of 1944 through 1963 was in the heart of both the industrial revolution and the birth of the Baby Boom generation. Today, we are mired in extreme volatility with frequent periods of boom and bust at the same time we are witnessing the beginning of the greatest retirement wave ever experienced within the U.S. economy.

To contrast these two time periods in respect to the recovery period is almost asinine as the external pressures from globalization and domestic unfunded liabilities did not exist or were irrelevant factors during the prior period.

To add insult to injury, U.S. domestic unfunded liabilities are currently estimated somewhere around $61.6 trillion due to items such as Social Security, Medicare and government pensions. The most concerning part of this pertains to the coming wave of retirement as the Baby Boom generation begins retiring and drawing on the unfunded Social Security for which they currently have entitlement. Over the long run, expenditures related to healthcare programs such as Medicare and Medicaid are projected to grow faster than the economy overall as the population matures.

To put unfunded liabilities into perspective, consider these as off-balance-sheet obligations similar to those of Enron. Although these are not listed as part of the national debt, they must be paid. These liabilities exist outside of the annual budgetary debt discussed. The difference between Enron and the U.S. unfunded liabilities is that if the U.S. government cannot come up with the funds to pay all these liabilities through revenue generation, they will print the money necessary to pay the debt.

WHAT DOES THE SOLUTION LOOK LIKE?

Unfortunately, the general public is in a no-win situation for this solution to the problem. Printing money does not bode well for economic growth. This creates inflationary pressures that devalue the U.S. dollar and make everyone less wealthy. Cutting the entitlements that compose this liability leaves millions of people without benefits they have come to expect. The only other option, and one that the government knows all too well, is increasing taxes. In fact, according to a Congressional Budget Office paper issued in 2004:

"The term 'unfunded liability' has been used to refer to a gap between the government's projected financial commitment under a particular program and the revenues that are expected to be available to fund that commitment. But no government obligation can be truly considered 'unfunded' because of the U.S. government's sovereign power to tax—which is the ultimate resource to meet its obligations."

A balanced budget will be required at some point and with this will come higher taxes. We have uncertainty surrounding tax rates and how high they will go. At that time, extensions put in place in December 2010 on Bush-era tax cuts are set to expire. We are likely to see some tax increases at this point. Whether it is only on the top earners or unilaterally across all income levels is yet to be seen, but an increase of some sort will most certainly occur.

How do you prepare? Why spend so much time reassuring you that taxes will increase? Because you have an opportunity to take action. Now is the time to prepare for what will come and structure countermeasures for the good, the bad and the ugly of each of these legislative nightmares through tax-advantaged retirement planning.

You make more money by saving on taxes than you do by making more money. The simplistic logic of the statement makes sense when you discover it takes $1.50 in earnings to put that same dollar, saved in taxes, back in your pocket.

As simple as it sounds, it is much more difficult to execute. Most people fail to put together a plan as they near retirement, beginning with a simple cash flow budget. If you have not analyzed your proposed income streams and expenses, you could not possibly have taken the time to position these cash flows and other events into a tax-preferred plan.

Most people will state that they have a plan and, thus, do not need any further assistance in this area. The truth in most instances is that people could not show you their plan, and among the few that could, most would not be able to show you how they have executed it. In this regard, they might as well be Richard Nixon stating, "I am not a crook" for as much as they state, "I have a plan." The truth lies in waiting. As we approach or begin retirement, we should look at what cash flows we will have. Do we have a pension? How about Social Security? How much additional cash flow am I going to need to draw from my assets to maintain the lifestyle that I desire?

We spend our whole lives saving and accumulating wealth but spend so little time determining how to distribute this accumulation so as to retain it. We need to make sure we have the appropriate diversification of taxable versus non-taxable assets to complement our distribution strategy.

THE BENEFITS OF DIVERSIFICATION

Heading into retirement, we should be situated with a diversified tax landscape. The point to spending our whole lives accumulating wealth is not to see the size of the number on paper, but rather to be an exercise in how much we put in our pocket after removing it from the paper. To truly understand tax diversification, we must understand what types of money exist and how each of these will be treated during accumulation and, most importantly, during distribution. The following is a brief summary:

1. Free money
2. Tax-advantaged money
3. Tax-deferred money
4. Taxable money
   a. Ordinary income
   b. Capital gains and qualified dividends

FREE MONEY

Free money is the best kind of money regardless of tax treatment because, in the end, you have more money than you would have otherwise. Many employers will provide contributions toward employee retirement accounts to offer additional employment benefits and encourage employees to save for their own retirement. With this, employers often will offer a matching contribution in which they contribute up to a certain percentage of an employee's salary (generally three to five percent) toward that employee's retirement account when the employee contributes to their retirement account as well. For example, if an employee earns $50,000 annually and contributes three percent ($1,500) to their retirement account annually, the employer will also contribute three percent ($1,500) to the employee's account. That is

$1,500 in free money. Take all you can get! Bear in mind that any employer contribution to a 401(k) will still be subject to taxation when withdrawn.

TAX-ADVANTAGED MONEY

Tax-advantaged money is the next best thing to free money. Although you have to earn tax-advantaged money, you do not have to give part of it away to Uncle Sam. Tax-advantaged money comes in three basic forms that you can utilize during your lifetime; four if prison inspires your future, but we are not going to discuss that option.

One of the most commonly known forms of tax-advantaged money is municipal bonds, which earn and pay interest that could be tax-advantaged on the federal level, or state level, or both. There are several caveats that should be discussed with regard to the notion of tax-advantaged income from municipal bonds. First, you will notice that tax-advantaged has several flavors from the state and federal perspective. This is because states will generally tax the interest earned on a municipal bond unless the bond is offered from an entity located within that state. This severely limits the availability of completely tax-advantaged municipal bonds and constrains underlying risk and liquidity factors. Second, municipal bond interest is added back into the equation for determining your modified adjusted gross income (MAGI) for Social Security. This could push your income above a threshold and subject a portion of your Social Security income to taxation.

In effect, if this interest subjects some other income to taxation then this interest is truly being taxed.

Last, municipal bond interest may be excluded from the regular federal tax system, but it is included for determining tax under the alternative minimum tax (AMT) system. In its basic form, the AMT system is a separate tax system that applies if the tax computed under AMT exceeds the tax computed under the regular tax system. The difference between these two computations is the alternative minimum tax.

TAX-ADVANTAGED MONEY: ROTH IRA

Roth accounts are probably the single greatest tax asset that has come from Congress outside of life insurance. They are well known but rarely used. Roth IRAs were first established by the Taxpayer Relief Act of 1997 and named after Senator William Roth, the chief sponsor of the legislation. Roth accounts are simply an account in the form of an individual retirement account or an employer sponsored retirement account that allows for tax-advantaged growth of earnings and, thus, tax-advantaged income.

The main difference between a Roth and a traditional IRA or employer-sponsored plan lies in the timing of the taxation. We are all very familiar with the typical scenario of putting money away for retirement through an employer plan, whereby they deduct money from our paychecks and put it directly into a retirement account. This money is taken out before taxes are calculated, meaning we do not pay tax on those earnings today. A Roth account, on the other hand, takes the money after the taxes have been removed and puts it into the retirement account, so we do pay tax on the money today. The other significant difference between these two is taxation during distribution in later years. Regarding our traditional retirement accounts, when we take the money out later it is added to our ordinary income and is taxed accordingly. Additionally, including this in our income subjects us to the consequences mentioned above for municipal bonds with Social Security taxation, AMT, as well as higher Medicare premiums. A Roth on the other hand is distributed tax-advantaged and does not contribute toward negative impact items such as Social Security taxation, AMT, or Medicare premium increases. It essentially comes back to us without tax and other obligations.

The best way to view the difference between the two accounts is to look at the life of a farmer. A farmer will buy seed, plant it in the ground, grow the crops and harvest it later for sale. Typically, the farmer would only pay tax on the crops that have been harvested and sold. But if you were the farmer, would you rather pay tax on the $5,000 of seed that you plant today or the $50,000 of crops harvested later? The obvious answer is $5,000 of seed today. The truth to the matter is that you are a farmer, except you plant dollars into your retirement account instead of seeds into the earth.

So why doesn't everyone have a Roth retirement account if things are so simple? There are several reasons, but the single greatest reason has been the constraints on contributions. If you earned over certain thresholds (MAGI over $125,000 single and $183,000 joint for 2012), you were not eligible to make contributions, and until last year, if your modified adjusted gross income (MAGI) was over $100,000 (single or joint), you could not convert a traditional IRA to a Roth. Outside these contribution limits, most people save for retirement through their employers and most employers do not offer Roth options in their plans. The reason behind this is because Roth accounts are not that well understood and people have been educated to believe that saving on taxes today is the best possible course of action.

TAX-ADVANTAGED MONEY: LIFE INSURANCE

As previously mentioned, the single greatest tax asset that has come from Congress outside of life insurance is the Roth account. Life insurance is the little-known or little-discussed tax asset that holds some of the greatest value in your financial history both during life and upon death. It is by far the best tax-advantaged device available. We traditionally view life insurance as a way to protect our loved ones from financial ruin upon our demise and it should be noted that everyone who cares about someone should have life insurance. Purchasing a life insurance policy ensures that our loved ones will receive income from the life insurance company to help them pay our final expenses and carry on with their lives without us comfortably when we die. The best part of the life insurance windfall is the fact that nobody will have to pay tax on the money received. This is the single greatest tax-advantaged device available, but it has one downside, we do not get to use it. Only our heirs will.

The little known and discussed part of life insurance is the cash value build-up within whole life and universal life (permanent) policies. Life insurance is not typically seen as an investment vehicle for building wealth and retirement planning, although we should discuss briefly why this thought process should be re-evaluated. Permanent life insurance is generally misconceived as something that is very expensive for a wealth accumulation vehicle because there are mortality charges (fees for the death benefit) that detract from the available returns. Furthermore, those returns do not yield as much as the stock market over the long run. This is why many times you will hear the phrase "buy term and invest the rest," where "term" refers to term insurance.

Let us take a second to review two terms just used in regard to life insurance: term and permanent. Term insurance is an idea with which most people are familiar. You purchase a certain death benefit that will go to your heirs upon death and this policy will be in effect for a certain number of years, typically 10 to 20 years. The 10 to 20 years is the term of the policy and once you have reached that end you no longer have insurance unless you purchase another policy.

Permanent insurance on the other hand has no term involved. It is permanent as long as the premiums continue to be paid. Permanent insurance generally initially has higher premiums than term insurance for the same amount of death benefit coverage and it is this difference that is referred to when people say "invest the rest."

Simply speaking there are significant differences between these two policies that are not often considered when providing a comparative analysis of the numbers. One item that gets lost in the fray when comparing term and permanent insurance is that term usually expires before death. In fact, insurance studies show less than one percent of all term policies pay out death benefit claims. The issue arises when the term expires and the desire to have more insurance is still present.

A term policy with the same benefit will be much more expensive than the original policy and, many times, life events occur, such as cancer or heart conditions, which makes it impossible to acquire another policy and leaves your loved ones unprotected and tax-advantaged legacy planning out of the equation.

Another aspect and probably the most important piece in consideration of the future of taxation is the fact that permanent insurance has a cash accumulation value. Two aspects stand out with the cash accumulation value. First, as the cash accumulation value increases the death benefit will also increase whereas term insurance remains level. Second, this cash accumulation offers value to you during your lifetime rather than to your heirs upon death. The cash accumulation value can be used for tax-advantaged income during your lifetime through policy loans. Most importantly, this tax-advantaged income is available during retirement for distribution planning, all while offering the same typical financial protection to your heirs.

TAX-DEFERRED MONEY

Tax-deferred money is the type of money with which most of people are familiar, but we also briefly reviewed the idea above. Tax-deferred money is typically our traditional IRA, employer sponsored retirement plan or a non-qualified annuity. Essentially, you put money into an investment vehicle that will accumulate in value over time and you do not pay taxes on the earnings that grow these accounts until you distribute them. Once the money is distributed, taxes must be paid. However, the same negative consequences exist with regard to additional taxation and expense in other areas as previously discussed. The cash accumulation value can be used for tax-advantaged income.

TAXABLE MONEY

Taxable money is everything else and is taxable today, later or whenever it is received. These four types of money come down to two distinct classifications: taxable and tax-free. The greatest difference when comparing taxable and tax-advantaged income is a function of how much money we keep after tax. For help in determining what the differences should be, excluding outside factors such as Social Security taxation and AMT, a tax equivalent yield should be used.

TAX-ADVANTAGED IN THE REAL WORLD

To put the tax equivalent yield into perspective, let us look at an example:

> » *Bob and Mary are currently retired, living on Social Security and interest from investments and falling within the 25 percent tax bracket. They have a substantial portion of their investments in municipal bonds yielding 6 percent, which is quite comforting in today's market. The tax equivalent yield they would need to earn from a taxable investment would be 8 percent, a 2 percent gap that seems almost impossible given current market volatility. However, something that has never been put into perspective is that the interest from their municipal bonds is subject to taxation on their Social Security benefits (at 21.25 percent). With this, the yield on*

their municipal bonds would be 4.725 percent, and the taxable equivalent yield falls to 6.3 percent, leaving a gap of only 1.575 percent.

In the end, most people spend their lives accumulating wealth through the best, if not the only vehicle they know, a tax-deferred account. This account is most likely a 401(k) or 403(b) plan offered through our employer and may be supplemented with an IRA that was established at one point or another. As the years go by, people blindly throw money into these accounts in an effort to save for a retirement that we someday hope to reach.

The truth is, most people have an age selected for when they would like to retire, but spend their lives wondering if they will ever be able to actually quit working. To answer this question, you must understand how much money you will have available to contribute toward your needs. ***In other words, you need to know what your after-tax income will be during this period.***

All else being equal, it would not matter if you put your money into a taxable, tax-deferred or tax-advantaged account as long as income tax rates never change and outside factors are never an event. The net amount you receive in the end will be the same.

Unfortunately, this will never be the case. We already know that taxes will increase in the future, meaning we will likely see higher taxes in retirement than during our peak earning years.

Regardless, saving for retirement in any form is a good thing as it appears from all practical perspectives that future government benefits will be cut and taxes will increase. You have the ability to plan today for efficient tax diversification and maximization of our after-tax dollars during your distribution years.

CHAPTER 11 RECAP //

- Diversifying your taxable and non-taxable assets can complement your income distribution strategy.
- Retirement savings plans can be tax-deferred or tax-advantaged. Both can be useful when preparing for retirement. It is important to find the right balance for your income needs.

12

MANAGE YOUR IRA

Good people come from Kentucky. My grandfather David Herstle Jones was born in Kentucky in 1897. Unfortunately he passed away in 1969. Another good Kentuckian was Louis Brandeis. Louis Brandeis provides one of the best examples illustrating how tax planning works. Brandeis was Associate Justice on the Supreme Court of the United States from 1916 to 1939. Born in Louisville, Kentucky, Brandeis was an intelligent man with a touch of country charm. He described tax planning this way:

"I live in Alexandria, Virginia. Near the Court Chambers, there is a toll bridge across the Potomac. When in a rush, I pay the dollar toll and get home early. However, I usually drive outside the downtown section of the city and cross the Potomac on a free bridge.

The bridge was placed outside the downtown Washington, D.C. area to serve a useful social service—getting drivers to drive the extra mile and help alleviate congestion during the rush hour.

If I went over the toll bridge and through the barrier without paying a toll, I would be committing tax evasion.

If I drive the extra mile and drive outside the city of Washington to the free bridge, I am using a legitimate, logical and suitable method of tax avoidance, and I am performing a useful social service by doing so."

*The tragedy is that **few people know that the free bridge exists.***

Like Brandeis, most American taxpayers have options when it comes to "crossing the Potomac," so to speak. It's a financial planner's job to tell you what options are available. You can wait until March to file your taxes, at which time you might pay someone to report and pay the government a larger portion of your income. However, you could instead file before the end of the year, work with your financial professional and incorporate a tax plan as part of your overall financial planning strategy. Filing later is like crossing the toll bridge. Tax planning is like crossing the free bridge.

Which would you rather do?

The answer to this question is easy. Most people want to save money and pay less in taxes. What makes this situation really difficult in real life, however, is that the signs along the side of the road that direct us to the free bridge are not that clear. To normal Americans, and to plenty of people who have studied it, the U.S. tax code is easy to get lost in. There are all kinds of rules, exceptions to rules, caveats and conditions that are difficult to understand, or even to know about. What you really need to know is your options and the bottom line impacts of those options. No one should pay more than their fair share of taxes…right?

ROTH IRA CONVERSIONS

The attractive qualities of Roth IRAs may have prompted you to explore the possibility of moving some of your assets into a Roth account. Another important difference between the accounts is how they treat Required Minimum Distributions (RMDs). When you turn 70 ½ years old, you are required to take a minimum amount of money out of a traditional IRA. This amount is your RMD. It is treated as taxable income. Roth IRAs, however, do not have RMDs, and their distributions are not taxable. Quite a deal, right?

While having a Roth IRA as part of your portfolio is a good idea, converting assets to a Roth IRA can pose some challenges, depending on what kinds of assets you want to transfer.

One common option is the conversion of a traditional IRA to a Roth IRA. You may have heard about converting your IRA to a Roth IRA, but you might not know the full net result on your income. The main difference between the two accounts is that the growth of investments within a traditional IRA is not taxed until income is withdrawn from the account, whereas taxes are charged on contribution amounts to a Roth IRA, not withdrawals. The problem, however, is that when assets are removed from a traditional IRA, even if the assets are being transferred to a Roth IRA account, taxes apply.

There are a lot of reasons to look at Roth conversions. People have a lot of money in IRAs, up to multiple millions of dollars. Even with $500,000, when they turn 70 ½ years old, their RMD is going to be approximately $18,000, and they have to take that out whether they want to or not. It's a tax issue. Essentially, if you will be subject to high RMDs, it could have impacts on how much of your Social Security is taxable, and on your tax bracket.

By paying taxes now instead of later on assets in a Roth IRA, you can realize tax-advantaged growth. You pay once and you're done paying. Your heirs are done paying. It's a powerful tool. Here's a simple example to show you how powerful it can be:

Imagine that you pay to convert a traditional IRA to a Roth. You have decided that you want to put the money in a vehicle that gives you a tax-advantaged income option down the road. If you pay a 25 percent tax on that conversion and the Roth IRA then doubles in value over the next 10 years, you could look at your situation as only having paid 12.5 percent tax.

The prospect of tax-advantaged income is a tempting one. While you have to pay a conversion tax to transfer your assets, you also have turned taxable income into tax free retirement money that you can let grow as long as you want without being required to withdraw it.

There are options, however, that address this problem. Much like the Brandeis story, there may be a "free bridge" option for many investors.

Your financial professional will likely tell you that it is not a matter of whether or not you should perform a Roth IRA conversion, it is a matter of how much you should convert and when.

Here are some of the things to consider before converting to a Roth IRA:

If you make a conversion before you retire, you may end up paying higher taxes on the conversion because it is likely that you are in some of your highest earning years, placing you in the highest tax bracket of your life. It is possible that a better strategy would be to wait until after you retire, a time when you may have less taxable income, which would place you in a lower tax bracket.

Many people opt to reduce their work hours from fulltime to part-time in the years before they retire. If you have pursued this option, your income will likely be lower, in turn lowering your tax rate.

The first years that you draw Social Security benefits can also be years of lower reported income, making it another good time frame in which to convert to a Roth IRA.

One key strategy to handling a Roth IRA conversion is to **always be able to pay the cost of the tax conversion with outside money**. Structuring your tax year to include something like a significant deduction can help you offset the conversion tax. This way you aren't forced to take the money you need for taxes from the value of the IRA. The reason taxes apply to this maneuver is because when you withdraw money from a traditional IRA, it is treated as taxable income by the IRS. Your financial professional, with the help of the CPAs at their firm, may be able to provide you with options like after-tax money, itemized deductions or other situations that can pose effective tax avoidance options.

Some examples of avoiding Roth IRA conversions taxes include:

- *Using medical expenses that are above 10 percent of your Adjusted Gross Income.* If you have health care costs that you can list as itemized deductions, you can convert an amount of income from a traditional IRA to a Roth IRA that is offset by the deductible amount. Essentially, deductible medical expenses negate the taxes resulting from recording the conversion.

- *Individuals, usually small business owners, who are dealing with a Net Operating Loss (NOL).* If you have NOLs, but aren't able to utilize all of them on your tax return, you can carry them forward to offset the taxable income from the taxes on income you convert to a Roth IRA.

- *Charitable giving.* If you are charitably inclined, you can use the amount of your donations to reduce the amount of taxable income you have during that year. By matching the amount you convert to a Roth IRA to the amount your taxable income was reduced by charitable giving, you can essentially avoid taxation on the conversion. You may decide to double your donations to a charity in one year, giving them two years' worth of donations in order to offset the Roth IRA conversion tax on this year's tax return.

- *Investments that are subject to depletion.* Certain investments can kick off depletion expenses. If you make an investment and are subject to depletion expenses, they can be deducted and used to offset a Roth IRA conversion tax.

Not all of the above scenarios work for everyone, and there are many other options for offsetting conversion taxes. The point is that you have options, and your financial professional and tax professional can help you understand those options.

If you have a traditional IRA, Roth conversions are something you should look at. As you approach retirement you should consider your options and make choices that keep more of your money in your pocket, not the government's.

ADDITIONAL TAX BENEFITS OF ROTH IRAS

Not only do Roth IRAs provide you with tax-advantaged growth, they also give you a tax diversified landscape that allows you to maximize your distributions. Chances are that no matter the circumstances, you will have taxed income and other assets subject to taxation. *But if you have a Roth IRA, you have the unique ability to manage your Adjusted Gross Income (AGI), because you have a tax-advantaged income option!*

Converting to a Roth IRA can also help you preserve and build your legacy. Because Roth IRAs are exempt from RMDs, after you make a conversion from a traditional IRA, your Roth account can grow tax-advantaged for another 15, 20 or 25 years and it can be used as tax-advantaged income by your heirs. It is important to note, however, that non-spousal beneficiaries do have to take

RMDs from a Roth IRA, or choose to stretch it and draw tax-advantaged income out of it over their lifetime.

TO CONVERT OR NOT TO CONVERT?

Conversions aren't only for retirees. You can convert at any time. Your choice should be based on your individual circumstances and tax situation. Sticking with a traditional IRA or converting to a Roth, again, depends on your individual circumstances, including your income, your tax bracket and the amount of deductions you have each year.

Is it better to have a Roth IRA or traditional IRA? It depends on your individual circumstance. Some people don't mind having taxable income from an IRA. Their income might not be very high and their RMD might not bump their tax bracket up, so it's not as big a deal. A similar situation might involve income from Social Security. Social Security benefits are taxed based on other income you are drawing. If you are in a position where none or very little of your Social Security benefit is subject to taxes, paying income tax on your RMD may be very easy.

> » *There are also situations where leveraging taxable income from a traditional IRA can work to your advantage come tax time. For example, Darrel and Linda dream of buying a boat when they retire. It is something they have looked forward to their entire marriage. In addition to the savings and investments that they created to supply them with income during retirement, which includes a traditional IRA, they have also saved money for the sole purpose of purchasing a boat once they stop working.*
>
> *When the time comes and they finally buy the boat of their dreams, they pay an additional $15,000 in sales taxes that year because of the large purchase. Because they are retired and earning less money, the deductions they used to be able to*

realize from their income taxes are no longer there. The high amount of sales taxes they paid on the boat puts them in a position where they could benefit from taking taxable income from a traditional IRA.

When Darrel and Linda's financial professional learns about their purchase, he immediately contacts a CPA at his firm to run the numbers. They determine that by taking a $15,000 distribution from their IRA, they could fulfill their income needs to offset the $15,000 sales tax deduction that they were claiming due to the purchase of their boat. In the end, they pay zero taxes on their income distribution from their IRA.

The moral of the story? ***Having a tax diversified landscape gives you options.*** Having capital assets that can be liquidated, tax-advantaged income options and sources that can create capital gains or capital losses will put you in a position to play your cards right no matter what you want to accomplish with your taxes. The ace up your sleeve is your financial professional and the CPAs they work with. Do yourself a favor and *plan* your taxes instead of *reporting* them!

CHAPTER 12 RECAP //

- You make more money by saving on taxes than you do by making more money. This simple concept becomes extremely valuable to people in retirement and those living on fixed incomes.

- When you report your taxes, you are paying to record history. When you *plan* your taxes with a financial professional, you are proactively finding the best options for your tax return.

- The future of U.S. taxation is uncertain. You know what the tax rate and landscape is today, but you won't tomorrow. The only thing you can really count on is the trend of increasing taxation.

- Look for the "free bridge" option in your tax strategy.

- Converting from a traditional to a Roth IRA can provide you with tax-advantaged retirement income.

- Converting to a Roth IRA can also help you preserve and build your legacy.

- There are many ways to reduce your taxes. Being smart about your Roth IRA conversion is one of the main ways to do so.

13
PROTECT YOUR LEGACY

Gordon Maxwell was 70 years old. He was one of the lucky few who had a pension, thanks to his lifelong career with the railroad, and he had also been able to put away an additional $250,000 IRA. Thanks to his pension, Gordon didn't need his IRA RMD when he turns 70.5. In fact, unless something unexpected comes up, Gordon thought he wouldn't ever need his RMDs. He hoped to be able to leave something to his two daughters, and that IRA was the cornerstone of his legacy plan. After meeting with his financial professional, Gordon knew his plan would work.

Gordon's financial professional suggested that he use his RMDs, which amounted to $12,000 every year, to purchase a $450,000 life insurance policy, naming his daughters as the beneficiaries. When he passes away, his daughters will receive a legacy almost twice as large as Gordon's IRA. But equally important, Gordon still has his IRA and his RMDs if he needs them. He can also access the cash value of *his life insurance policy if he has an unexpected need. The big bonus however, is the fact that his daughters won't have to pay tax on the $450,000 death benefit, where they would have had to pay taxes on the inherited IRA monies.*

If you're like most people, planning your estate isn't on the top of your list of things to do. Planning your income needs for retirement, managing your assets and just living your life without worrying about how your estate will be handled when you are gone make legacy planning less than attractive for a Saturday afternoon task. The fact of the matter, however, is that if you don't plan your legacy, someone else will. That someone else is usually a combination of the IRS and other government entities: lawyers, executors, courts, and accountants. Who do you think has the best interests of your beneficiaries in mind?

Today, there is more consideration given to planning a legacy than just maximizing your estate. When most people think about an estate, it may seem like something only the very wealthy have: a stately manor or an enormous business. But a legacy is something else entirely. A legacy is more than the sum total of the financial assets you have accumulated. It is the lasting impression you make on those you leave behind. The dollar and cents are just a small part of a legacy.

A legacy encompasses the stories that others tell about you, shared experiences and values. An estate may pay for college tuition, but a legacy may inform your grandchildren about the importance of higher education and self-reliance.

A legacy may also contain family heirlooms or items of emotional significance. It may be a piece of art your great-grandmother painted, family photos, or a childhood keepsake.

When you go about planning your legacy, certainly explore strategies that can maximize the financial benefit to the ones you care about. But also take the time to ensure that you have organized the whole of your legacy, and let that be a part of the last gift you leave.

Many people avoid planning their legacy until they feel they must. Something may change in your life, like the birth of a grandchild, the diagnosis of a serious health problem, or the death of a close friend or loved one. Waiting for tragedy to strike in order to get your affairs in order is not the best course of action. The emotional stress of that kind of situation can make it hard to make patient, thoughtful decisions. Taking the time to create a premeditated and thoughtful legacy plan will assure that your assets will be transferred where and when you want them when the time comes.

Be proactive, not reactive. This approach will not only give you less stress, it will give you better results.

THE BENEFITS OF PLANNING YOUR LEGACY
The distribution of your assets, whether in the form of property, stocks, Individual Retirement Accounts, 401(k)s or liquid assets, can be a complicated undertaking if you haven't left clear instructions about how you want them handled. Not having a plan will cost more money and take more time, leaving your loved ones to wait (sometimes for years) and receive less of your legacy than if you had a clear plan.

Planning your legacy will help your assets be transferred with little delay and little confusion. Instead of leaving decisions about how to distribute your estate to your family, attorneys or financial professionals, preserve your legacy and your wishes by drafting a clear plan at an early age.

And while you know all that, it can still be hard to sit down and do it. It reminds you that life is short, and the relatively complicated nature of sorting through your assets can feel like a daunting task. But one thing is for sure: ***it is impossible for your***

assets to be transferred or distributed the way you want at the end of your life if you don't have a plan.

Ask yourself:

- Are my assets up to date?
- Have my primary and contingent beneficiaries been clearly designated?
- Does my plan allow for restriction of a beneficiary?
- Does my legacy plan address minor children that I want to provide with income?
- Does my legacy plan allow for multi-generational payout?

Answers to these questions are critical if you want the final say in how your assets are distributed. In order to achieve your legacy goals, you need a plan.

MAKING A PLAN

Eventually, when your income need is filled and you have sufficient standby money to meet your need for emergencies, travel or other extra expenses you are planning for, whatever isn't used during your lifetime becomes your financial legacy. The money that you do not use during your lifetime will either go to loved ones, unloved ones, charity, or the IRS. The question is, who would you rather disinherit?

By having a legacy plan that clearly outlines your assets, your beneficiaries and your distribution goals, you can make sure that your money and property is ending up in the hands of the people you determine beforehand. Is it really that big of a deal? It absolutely is. Think about it. Without a clear plan, it is impossible for anyone to know if your beneficiary designations are current and reflect your wishes because you haven't clearly expressed who your beneficiaries are. You may have an idea of who you want your assets to go to, but without a plan, it is anyone's guess. It is also impossible to know if the titling of your assets is accurate unless you have gone through and determined whose name is on the titles. More importantly, *if you have not clearly and effectively communicated your desires regarding the planned distribution of your legacy, you and your family may end up losing a large part of it.*

As you can see, managing a legacy is more complicated than having an attorney read your will, divide your estate and write checks to your heirs. The additional issue of taxes, Family Maximum Benefit calculations and a host of other decisions rear their heads. Educating yourself about the best options for positioning your legacy assets is a challenging undertaking. Working with a financial professional who is versed in determining the most efficient and effective ways of preserving and distributing your legacy can save you time, money and strife.

So, how do you begin?

Making a Legacy Plan Starts with a Simple List. The first, and one of the largest, steps to setting up an estate plan with a financial professional that reflects your desires is creating a detailed inventory of your assets and debts (if you have any). You need to know what assets you have, who the beneficiaries are, how much they are worth and how they are titled. You can start by identifying and listing your assets. This is a good starting point for working with a financial professional who can then help you determine the detailed information about your assets that will dictate how they are distributed upon your death.

If you are particularly concerned about leaving your kids and grandkids a lifetime of income with minimal taxes, you will want to discuss a Stretch IRA option with your financial professional.

STRETCH IRAS: GETTING THE MOST OUT OF YOUR MONEY

In 1986, the U.S. Congress passed a law that allows for multi-generational distributions of IRA assets. This type of distribution is called a Stretch IRA because it stretches the distribution of the account out over a longer period of time to several beneficiaries. It also allows the account to continue accumulating value throughout your relatives' lifetimes. You can use a Stretch IRA as an income tool that distributes throughout your lifetime, your children's lifetimes and your grandchildren's lifetimes.

Stretch IRAs are an attractive option for those more concerned with creating income for their loved ones than leaving them with a lump sum that may be subject to a high tax rate. With traditional IRA distributions, non-spousal beneficiaries must generally take distributions from their inherited IRAs, whether transferred or not, within five years after the death of the IRA owner. An exception to this rule applies if the beneficiary elects to take distributions over his or her lifetime, which is referred to as stretching the IRA.

Let's begin by looking at the potential of stretching an IRA throughout multiple generations.

> *In this scenario, Mr. Cleaver has an IRA with a current balance of $350,000. If we assume a five percent annual rate of return, and a 28% tax rate, the Stretch IRA turned a $502,625 legacy into more than $1.5 million. Doubling the value of the IRA also provided Mr. Cleaver, his wife, two children and three grandchildren with income. Not choosing the stretch option would have cost nearly $800,000 and had impacts on six of Mr. Cleaver's loved ones.*

Unfortunately, many things may also play a role in failing to stretch IRA distributions. It can be tempting for a beneficiary to take a lump sum of money despite the tax consequences. Fortunately, if you want to solidify your plan for distribution, there are options that will allow you to open up an IRA and incorporate "spendthrift" clauses for your beneficiaries. This will ensure your legacy is stretched appropriately and to your specifications. Only certain insurance companies allow this option, and you will not find this benefit with any brokerage accounts. You need to work with a financial professional who has the appropriate relationship with an insurance company that provides this option.

CHAPTER 13 RECAP //

- Planning your estate is probably not at the top of your to-do list, but if you don't create a plan, chances are lawyers and the government will receive a much greater share of your legacy than your beneficiaries.
- Creating a plan for your legacy begins with a simple list: create a list of all of your assets and then work with your financial professional to plan how those assets will be distributed.
- Stretch IRAs offer a unique way to receive an income from your IRA while also leaving a lasting legacy for your heirs.

14

PREPARE YOUR LEGACY

David organized his assets long ago. He started planning his retirement early and made investment decisions that would meet his needs. With a combination of IRA to Roth IRA conversions, a series of income annuities and a well-planned money management strategy overseen by his financial professional, he easily filled his income gap and was able to focus on ways to accumulate his wealth throughout his retirement. He reorganized his Know So and Hope So Money as he got older. When David retired, he had an income plan created that allowed him to maximize his Social Security benefit. He even had enough to accumulate wealth during his retirement. At this point, David turned his attention to planning his legacy. He wanted to know how he could maximize the amount of his legacy he will pass on to his heirs.

David met with an attorney to draw up a will, but he quickly learned that while having a will was a good plan, it wasn't the most efficient way to distribute his legacy. In fact, relying solely on a will created several roadblocks.

The two main problems that arose for David were *Probate* and *Unintentional Disinheritance:*

Problem #1: Probate

Probate. Just speaking the word out loud can cause shivers to run down your spine. Probate's ugly reputation is well deserved. It can be a costly, time consuming process that diminishes your estate and can delay the distribution of your estate to your loved ones. Nasty stuff, by any measure. Unless you have made a clear legacy plan and discussed options for avoiding probate, it is highly likely that you have many assets that might pass through probate need- lessly. *If your will and beneficiary designations aren't correctly structured, some of these assets will go through the probate process, which can turn dollars into cents.*

If you have a will, probate is usually just a formality. There is little risk that your will won't be executed per your instructions. The problem arises when the costs and lengthy timeline that probate creates come into play. Probate proceedings are notori- ously expensive, lengthy and ponderous. A typical probate process identifies all of your assets and debts, pays any taxes and fees that you owe (including estate tax), pays court fees, and distributes your property and assets to your inheritors. This process usually takes at least a year, and can take even longer before your inheri- tors actually receive anything that you have left for them. For this reason, and because of the sometimes exorbitant fees that may be charged by lawyers and accountants during the process, probate has earned a nasty reputation.

Probate can also be a painstakingly public process. Because the probate process happens in court, the assets you own that go through a probate procedure become part of the public record.

While this may not seem like a big deal to some, other people don't want that kind of intimate information available to the public.

Additionally, if your estate is entirely distributed via your will, there is a risk that the money that your family may need to cover the costs of your medical bills, funeral expenses and estate taxes may be tied up in probate, which can last up to a year or more. While immediate family members may have the option of requesting immediate cash from your assets during probate to cover immediate health care expenses, taxes, and fees, that process comes with its own set of complications. Choosing alternative methods for distributing your legacy can make life easier for your loved ones and can help them claim more of your estate in a more timely fashion than traditional methods.

A simpler and less tedious approach is to avoid probate altogether by structuring your estate to be distributed outside of the probate process. Two common ways of doing this are by structuring your assets inside a life insurance plan, and by using individual retirement planning tools like IRAs that give you the option of designating a beneficiary upon your death.

Problem #2: Unintentionally Disinheriting Your Family

You would never want to unintentionally disinherit a loved one or loved ones because of confusion surrounding your legacy plan. Unfortunately, it happens. Why? This terrible situation is typically caused by a simple lack of understanding. In particular, mistakes regarding legacy distribution occur with regards to those whom people care for the most: their grandchildren.

One of the most important ways to plan for the inheritance of your grandchildren is by properly structuring the distribution of your legacy. Specifically, you need to know if your legacy is going to be distributed *per stirpes* or *per capita*.

Per Stirpes. *Per stirpes* is a legal term in Latin that means "by the branch." Your estate will be distributed *per stirpes* if you designate each branch of your family to receive an equal share of your estate. In the event that your children predecease you, their share will be distributed evenly between their children — your grandchildren.

Per Capita. *Per capita* distribution is different in that you may designate different amounts of your estate to be distributed to members of the same generation.

Per stirpes distribution of assets will follow the family tree down the line as the predecessor beneficiaries pass away. On the other hand, per capita distribution of assets ends on the branch of the family tree with the death of a designated beneficiary. For example, when your child passes away, in a per capita distribution, your grandchildren would not receive distributions from the assets that you designated to your child.

What the terms mean is not nearly as important as what they do, however. The reality is that improperly titled assets could accidentally leave your grandchildren disinherited upon the death of their parents. It's easy to check, and it's even easier to fix.

A simple way to remember the difference between the two types of distribution goes something like this: "*Stripes are forever and Capita is capped.*"

Another way to avoid complicated legacy distribution problems, and the probate process, is by leveraging a life insurance plan.

LIFE INSURANCE: AN IMPORTANT LEGACY TOOL

One of the most powerful legacy tools you can leverage is a good life insurance policy. Life insurance is a highly efficient legacy tool because it creates money when it is needed or desired the most. Over the years, life insurance has become less expensive, while it offers more features, and it provides longer guarantees.

There are many unique benefits of life insurance that ca
your beneficiaries get the most out of your legacy. Some of them
include:

- Providing beneficiaries with a tax-free, liquid asset.
- Covering the costs associated with your death.
- Providing income for your dependents.
- Offering an investment opportunity for your beneficiaries.
- Covering expenses such as tuition or mortgage down pay-
  ments for your children or grandchildren.

Very few people want life insurance, but nearly everyone wants
what it does. Life insurance is specifically, and uniquely, capable
of creating money when it is needed most. When a loved one
passes, no amount of money can remove the pain of loss. And
certainly, money doesn't solve the challenges that might arise with
losing someone important.

It has been said that when you have money, you have options.
When you don't have money, your options are severely limited.
You might imagine a life insurance policy can give your family
and loved ones options that would otherwise be impossible.

> » Ben spent the last 20 years building a small business. In so
> many ways, it is a family business. Each of his three children,
> Maddie, Ruby and Edward, worked in the shop part-time
> during high school. But after all three attended college, only
> Maddie returned to join her father, and eventually will run
> the business full-time when Ben retires.
>
> Ben is able to retire comfortably on Social Security and
> on-going income from the shop, but the business is nearly his
> entire financial legacy. It is his wish that Maddie own the
> business outright, but he also wants to leave an equal legacy
> to each of his three children.

There is no simple way to divide the business into thirds and still leave the business intact for Maddie.

Ben ends up buying a life insurance policy to make up the difference. Ruby and Edward will receive their share of an inheritance in cash from the life insurance policy and Maddie will be able to inherit the business intact.

Ben is able to accomplish his goals, treat all three children equitably and leave Maddie the business she helped to build.

If you have a life insurance policy but you haven't looked at it in a while, you may not know how it operates, how much it is worth and how it will be distributed to your beneficiaries. You may also need to update your beneficiaries on your policy. In short, without a comprehensive review of your policy, you don't really know where the money will go or to whom it will go.

If you don't have a life insurance policy but are looking for options to maintain and grow your legacy, speaking with a professional can show you the benefits of life insurance. Many people don't consider buying a life insurance policy until some event in their life triggers it, like the loss of a loved one, an accident or a health condition.

BENEFITS OF LIFE INSURANCE

Life insurance is a useful and secure tool for contingency planning, ensuring that your dependents receive the assets that you want them to have, and for meeting the financial goals you have set for the future. While it bears the name "Life Insurance," it is, in reality, a diverse financial tool that can meet many needs. The main function of a life insurance policy is to provide financial assets for your survivors. Life insurance is particularly efficient at achieving this goal because it provides a tax-advantaged lump sum of money in the form of a death benefit to your beneficiary or beneficiaries. That financial asset can be used in a number of ways. It can be structured as an investment to provide income for your spouse or children, it can pay down debts, and it can be used to cover estate taxes and other costs associated with death.

Tax liabilities on the estate you leave behind are inevitable. Capital property, for instance, is taxed at its fair market value at the time of your death, unless that property is transferred to your spouse. If the property has appreciated during the time you owned it, taxation on capital gains will occur. Registered Retirement Savings Plans (RRSPs) and other similarly structured assets are also included as taxable income unless transferred to a beneficiary as well. Those are just a few examples of how an estate can become subject to a heavy tax burden. The unique benefits of a life insurance policy provide ways to handle this tax burden, solving any liquidity problems that may arise if your family members want to hold onto an illiquid asset, such as a piece of property or an investment. Life insurance can provide a significant amount of money to a family member or other beneficiary, and that money is likely to remain exempt from taxation or seizure.

One of life insurance's most important benefits is that it is not considered part of the estate of the policy holder. The death benefit that is paid by the insurance company goes exclusively to the beneficiaries listed on the policy. This shields the proceeds of the policy from fees and costs that can reduce an estate, including probate proceedings, attorneys' fees and claims made by creditors. The distribution of your life insurance policy is also unaffected by delays of the estate's distribution, like probate. Your beneficiaries will get the proceeds of the policy in a timely fashion, regardless of how long it takes for the rest of your estate to be settled.

Investing a portion of your assets in a life insurance policy can also protect that portion of your estate from creditors. If you owe money to someone or some entity at the time of your death, a creditor is not able to claim any money from a life insurance policy or an annuity, for that matter. As an exception to this rule, if you had already used the life insurance policy as collateral against a loan. If a large portion of the money you want to dedicate to your legacy is sitting in a savings account, investment or other liquid form, creditors may be able to receive their claim on it before your beneficiaries get anything; that is, if there's anything left. A life insurance policy protects your assets from creditors and ensures that your beneficiaries get the money that you intend them to have.

HOW MUCH LIFE INSURANCE DO YOU NEED?

Determining the type of policy and the amount right for you depends on an analysis of your needs. A financial professional can help you complete a needs analysis that will highlight the amount of insurance that you require to meet your goals. This type of personalized review will allow you to determine ways to continue providing income for your spouse or any dependents you may have. A financial professional can also help you calculate the amount of income that your policy should replace to meet the needs of your beneficiaries and the duration of the distribution of that income.

You may also want to use your life insurance policy to meet any expenses associated with your death. These can include funeral costs, fees from probate and legal proceedings, and taxes. You may also want to dedicate a portion of your policy proceeds to help fund tuition or other expenses for your children or grandchildren. You can buy a policy and hope it covers all of those costs, or you can work with a professional who can calculate exactly how much insurance you need and how to structure it to meet your goals. Which would you rather do?

AVOIDING POTENTIAL SNAGS

There are benefits to having life insurance supersede the direction given in a will or other estate plan, but there are also some potential snags that you should address to meet your wishes. For example, if your will instructs that your assets be divided equally between your two children but your life insurance beneficiary is listed as just one of the children, the assets in the life insurance policy will only be distributed to the child listed as the beneficiary. The beneficiary designation of your life insurance supersedes your will's instruction. This is important to understand when designating beneficiaries on a policy you purchase. Work with a professional to make sure that your beneficiaries are accurately listed on your assets, especially your life insurance policies.

USING LIFE INSURANCE TO BUILD YOUR LEGACY

Depending on your goals, there are strategies you can use that could multiply how much you leave behind. Life insurance is one of the most surefire and efficient investment tools for building a substantial legacy that will meet your financial goals.

Here is a brief overview of how life insurance can boost your legacy:

- Life insurance provides an immediate increase in your legacy.
- It provides an income tax-advantaged death benefit for your beneficiaries.
- A good life insurance policy has the opportunity to accumulate value over time.
- It may have an option to include long-term care (LTC) or chronic illness benefits should you require them.

If your Green Money income needs for retirement are met and you have Yellow Money assets that will provide for your future expenses, you may have extra assets that you want to earmark as legacy funds. By electing to invest those assets into a life insurance policy, you can immediately increase the amount of your legacy. Remember, **life insurance allows you to transfer**

a tax-advantaged lump sum of money to your beneficiaries. It remains in your control during your lifetime, can provide for your long-term care needs and bypasses probate costs. And make no mistake, taxes can have a huge impact on your legacy. Not only that, income and assets from your legacy can have tax implications for your beneficiaries, as well.

Here's a brief overview of how taxes could affect your legacy and your beneficiaries:

- The higher your income, the higher the rate at which it is taxed.
- Withdrawals from qualified plans are taxed as income.
- What's more, when you leave a large qualified plan, it ends up being taxed at a high rate.
- If you left a $500,000 IRA to your child, they could end up owing as much as $140,000 in income taxes.
- However, if you could just withdraw $50,000 a year, the tax bill might only be $10,000 per year.

How could you use that annual amount to leave a larger legacy? Luckily, you can leverage a life insurance policy to avoid those tax penalties, preserving a larger amount of your legacy and freeing your beneficiaries from an added tax burden.

> » *When Brenda turned 70 years old, she decided it was time to look into life insurance policy options. She still feels young, but she remembers that her mother died in early 70s, and she wants to plan ahead so she can pass on some of her legacy to her grandchildren just like her grandmother did for her.*
>
> *Brenda doesn't really want to think about life insurance, but she does want the security, reliability and tax-advantaged distribution that it offers. She lives modestly, and her Social Security benefit meets most of her income needs. As the beneficiary of her late husband's Certificate of Deposit (CD), she*

has $100,000 in an account that she has never used and doesn't anticipate ever needing since her income needs were already met.

*After looking at several different investment options with a professional, Brenda decides that a Single Premium life insurance policy fits her needs best. She can buy the policy with a $100,000 one-time payment and she is guaranteed that it would provide more than the value of the contract to her beneficiaries. If she left the money in the CD, it would be subject to taxes. But for every dollar that she puts into the life insurance policy, her beneficiaries are guaranteed at least that dollar plus a death benefit, and all of it will be **tax-free!***

For $100,000, Brenda's particular policy offers a $170,000 death benefit distribution to her beneficiaries. By moving the $100,000 from a CD to a life insurance policy, Brenda increases her legacy by 70 percent. Not only that, she has also sheltered it from taxes, so her beneficiaries will be able to receive $1.70 for every $1.00 that she entered into the policy! While buying the policy doesn't allow her to use the money for herself, it does allow her family to benefit from her well-planned legacy.

MAKE YOUR WISHES KNOWN

Estate taxes used to be a much hotter topic in the mid-2000s when the estate tax limits and exclusions were much smaller and taxed at a higher rate than today. In 2008, estates valued at $2 million or more were taxed at 45 percent. Just two years later, the limit was raised to $5 million dollars taxed at 35 percent. The limit has continued to rise ever since. The limit applies to fewer people than before. Estate organization, however, is just as important as ever, and it affects everyone.

Ask yourself:
- Are your assets actually titled and held the way you think they are?
- Are your beneficiaries set up the way you think they should be?
- Have there been changes to your family or those you desire as beneficiaries?

There is more to your legacy beyond your property, money, investments and other assets that you leave to family members, loved ones and charities. Everyone has a legacy beyond money. You also leave behind personal items of importance, your values and beliefs, your personal and family history, and your wishes. Beyond a will and a plan for your assets, it is important that you make your wishes known to someone for the rest of your personal legacy. When it comes time for your family and loved ones to make decisions after you are gone, knowing your wishes can help them make decisions that honor you and your legacy, and give meaning to what you leave behind. Your professional can help you organize.

Think about your:
- Personal stories / recollections
- Values
- Personal items of emotional significance
- Financial assets

Do you want to make a plan to pass these things on to your family?

WORKING WITH A PROFESSIONAL

Part of using life insurance to your greatest advantage is selecting the policy and provider that can best meet your goals. Venturing into the jungle of policies, brokers and salespeople can be overwhelming, and can leave you wondering if you've made the best decision. Working with a trusted financial professional can help you cut through the red tape, the "sales-speak" and confusion to find a policy that meets your goals and best serves your desires for your money. If you already have a policy, a financial professional can help you review it and become familiar with the policy's premium, the guarantees the policy affords, its performance, and its features and benefits. A financial professional can also help you make any necessary changes to the policy.

> » *When Cheryl turned 88, her daughter finally convinced her to meet with a financial professional to help her organize her assets and get her legacy in order. Although Cheryl is reluctant to let a stranger in on her personal finances, she ends up very glad that she did.*
>
> *In the process of listing Cheryl's assets and her beneficiaries, her professional finds a man's name listed as the beneficiary of an old life insurance policy and annuity that she owns. It turns out, the man is Cheryl's ex-husband who is still alive. Had Cheryl passed away before her ex-husband, the annuity and any death benefits from the life insurance policy would have been passed on to her ex-husband. This does not reflect her latest wishes.*

Things change, relationships evolve and the way you would like your legacy organized needs to adapt to the changes that happen throughout your life. There may be a new child or grandchild in your family, or you may have been divorced or remarried. A professional will regularly review your legacy assets and ask you questions to make sure that everything is up to date and that the current organization reflects your current wishes.

CHAPTER 14 RECAP //

- You can structure your assets in ways that maximize distributions to your beneficiaries.
- Working with a financial professional can help ensure that many of your assets avoid the ponderous and expensive probate process.
- A financial professional can help review the details of the assets you have designated to be a part of your legacy and make sure that you aren't unintentionally disinheriting your heirs.
- Life insurance provides the distribution of tax-free, liquid assets to your beneficiaries.
- Investing in a life insurance policy can significantly build your legacy.
- Organizing your estate will allow you to make sure your wishes are properly carried through.
- You can take advantage of a "Stretch IRA" to provide income for you, your spouse and your beneficiaries throughout their lifetimes.
- Understand if your assets will be distributed *per stirpes* or *per capita*.
- Working with a financial professional can help you select the policy that best meets your needs, or can help you fine tune your existing policy to better reflect your desires and intentions.
- Be proactive, not reactive.

15

CHOOSE THE RIGHT TEAM

From the moment you dip your toes into the retirement planning pool to the point you start swimming laps, your assets organized, your income needs met, and your accumulation and legacy plans in place, working with a professional that you trust can make all the difference in how well your retirement reflects your desires.

It is important to know what you are looking for before taking the plunge. There are many people that would love to handle your money, but not everyone is qualified to handle it in a way that leads to a holistic approach to creating a solid retirement plan.

The distinction being made here is that you should look for someone that puts your interests first and actively wants to help you meet your goals and objectives. The right financial professionals will take your whole financial position into consideration.

They will make plans that adjust your risk exposure, invest in solutions that secure your desired income during retirement and create investment strategies that allow you to continue accumulating wealth during your retirement for you to use later or to contribute to your legacy. Financial solutions and investment options change, but the concepts that lie behind wise retirement planning are lasting. In the end, a financial professional's approach is designed for those serious about planning for retirement. *Can you say the same thing about the person who advises you about your financial life?*

It's easy to see how choosing a financial professional can be one of the most important decisions you can make in your life. Not only do they provide you with advice, they also manage the personal assets that supply your retirement income and contribute to your legacy. So, how do you find a good one?

HOW TO FIND A FINANCIAL PROFESSIONAL YOU CAN TRUST

Taking care to select a financial professional is one of the best things you can do for yourself and for your future. Your professional has influence and control of your investment decisions, making their role in your life more than just important. Your financial security and the quality of your retirement depend on the decisions, investment strategies and asset structuring that you and your professional create.

Working with a professional is different than calling up a broker when you want to buy or trade some stock. This isn't a decision that you can hand off to anyone else. You need to bring your time and attention to the table when it comes to finding someone with whom you can entrust your financial life. Separating the wheat from the chaff will take some work, but you'll be happy you did it.

While no one can tell you exactly who to choose or how to choose them, the following information can help you narrow the field:

You can start by asking your friends, family and colleagues for referrals. You will want to pay particular attention to the recommendations that you get from others who are in your similar financial situation and who have similar lifestyle choices. The professional for the CEO of your company may have a different skill-set than the skill-set of the professional befitting your cousin who has 3 kids and a Subaru like you. Do follow-up research on the Internet as well. Look up the people who have been recommended to you on websites like The National Ethics Association, The Better Business Bureau, and the like. These types of sites will show the work history, referrals and experience of the candidates that you find most attractive. You will also learn about the firms with or for whom they work. The investment philosophies and reputations of the companies they work for will tell you a lot about how they will handle your money.

The other side of the coin, however, is that everyone and their brother has a recommendation about how you should manage your money and who should manage it for you. From hot stock tips to "the best money manager in the state," people love to share good information that makes them look like they are in-the-know. Nobody wants to talk about the bad stock purchases they made, the times they lost money and the poor selections they made regarding financial professionals or stock brokers. If you decide to take a friend or family member's recommendation, make sure they have a substantial, long-term experience with the financial professional and that their glowing review isn't just based on a one-time "win."

You can also use online tools like the search function of the Financial Planning Association (http://www.fpanet. org/) and the National Association of Personal Financial professionals (http://

www.napfa.org/). Most of the professionals listed on these sites do not earn commissions from selling financial solutions, but are instead paid on a fee-only basis for their services. It is important to understand how your professional is being paid. It is generally considered preferable to work with a fee-based professional who will not have conflicts of interests between earning a commission and acting in your best interests.

Many professionals may also be brokers or dealers that can earn commissions on things like life insurance, certain types of annuities and disability insurance. These professionals have most likely intentionally overlapped their roles so that if their clients choose to purchase insurance or investment solutions that require a broker or dealer, those clients won't have to find an additional person to work with. Again, understanding the role of your professional will help you make your determination.

NARROWING THE FIELD

1. Decide on the Type of Professional with Whom You Want to Work. There are four basic kinds of financial professionals. Many professionals may play overlapping roles. It is important to know a professional's primary function, how they charge for their services and whether they are obligated to act in your best interest.

Registered representatives, better known as stockbrokers or bank / investment representatives, make their living by earning commissions on insurance products and investment services. Stockbrokers basically sell you things. The products from which they make the highest commission are sometimes the products that they recommend to their clients. If you want to make a simple transaction, such as buying or selling a particular stock, a registered representative can help you. Although registered representatives are licensed professionals, if you want to create a structured and planful approach to positioning your assets for retirement, you might want to consider continuing your search.

The term "planner" is often misused. It can refer to credible professionals who are CPAs, CFPs, LUTCFs, and ChFCs, or to your uncle's next-door neighbor who claims to have a lead on some undervalued stock about to be "discovered." A wide array of people may claim to be planners because there are no requirements to be a planner. The term financial planner, however, refers to someone who is properly registered as an investment advisor and serves as a fiduciary as described below.

Financial professionals are the diamonds in the rough. These Registered Investment Advisors are compensated on a fee basis. They do, however, often have licensure as stockbrokers or insurance agents, allowing them to earn commissions on certain transactions. More importantly, **financial professionals are financial fiduciaries, meaning they are required to make financial decisions in your best interest and reflecting your risk tolerance.** Investment Advisors are held to high ethical standards and are highly regarded in the financial industry. Financial professionals also often take a more comprehensive approach to asset management. These professionals are trained and credentialed to plan and coordinate their clients' assets in order to meet their goals or retirement and legacy planning. They are not focused on individual stocks, investments or markets. They look at the big picture, the whole enchilada.

Money managers are on par with financial professionals. However, they are often given explicit permission to make investment decisions without advanced approval by their clients.

Understanding who you are working with and what their title is the first step to planning your retirement. While each of the above-mentioned types of financial professionals can help you with aspects of your finances, it is **financial professionals** who have the most intimate role, the most objective investment strategies and the most unbiased mode of compensation for their services. A financial professional can also help you with the nonfinancial aspects of your legacy and can help you find ways to create a tax planning strategy to help you save money.

2. Be Objective. At the end of the day, you need to separate the weak from the strong. While you might want a strong personal rapport with your professional, or you may want to choose your professional for their personality and positive attitude, it is more important that you find someone who will give sage advice regarding achieving your retirement goals.

It can be helpful to use a process of elimination to narrow the field of potential professionals. Look into five or six potential leads and cross off your list the ones that don't meet your requirements until only one or two remain. Cross-check your remaining choices against the list of things you need from a professional. Make sure they represent a firm that has the investment tools and solutions that you desire, and make sure they have experience in retirement planning. That is, after all, the main goal.

Don't be afraid to investigate each of your candidates. You'll want to ask the same questions and look for the same information from everyone you consider so you can then compare them and discern which is best for you. You'll want to take a look at the specific credentials of each professional, their experience and competence, their ethics and fiduciary status, their history and track record, and a list of the services that they offer. The professionals who meet all or most of your qualifications are the ones you will contact for an interview.

Potential professionals should meet your qualifications in the following categories:

- *Credentials:* Look at their experience, the quality of their education, any associations to which they belong and certifications they have earned. Someone who has continued their professional education through ongoing certifications will be more up-to-date on current financial practices compared to someone who got their degree 25 years ago and hasn't done a thing since.

- *Practices:* Look at the track record of your candidates, how they are compensated for their services, the reports and analysis they offer, and their value added services.
- *Services:* Your professional must meet your needs. If you are planning your retirement, you should work with someone who offers services that help you to that end. You want someone who can offer planning, advice on investment strategies, ways to calculate risk, advice on insurance and annuities solutions, and ways to manage your tax strategy.
- *Ethics:* You want to work with someone who is above board and does things the right way. Vet them by checking their compliance record, current licensing, fiduciary status and, yes, even their criminal record. You never know!

It is definitely a bonus if you are able to work with a firm which has professionals in the "Big 4" areas of planning: Investment, Insurance, Tax, and Legal.

3. Ask for and Check References. Once you have selected two or three professionals that you want to meet, call or email them and ask for references. Every professional should be able to provide you with at least two or three names. In fact, they will probably be eager to share them with you. Most professionals rely on references for validation of their success, quality of services and likability. You should, however, take them with a grain of salt. You have no way to know whether or not references are a professional's friends or colleagues.

It is worth contacting references, however, to check for inconsistencies. Ask each reference the same set of questions to get the same basic information. How long have they been working with the professional? What kind of services have they used and were they happy with them? What type of financial planning did they use the professional for? Were they versed in the type of financial planning that you needed? You can also ask them direct questions to elicit candid responses. What was the full cost of the expenses that your professional charged you? Do the reports and statements you receive come from the same firm? Questions like these can help you get a sense of how well the reference knows their professional and whether or not they are a quality reference.

A good reference is a bit like icing on the cake. It's nice to have them, but nothing speaks louder than a good track record and quality experience. And remember that a good reference, while nice to hear, is relatively cheap. How many times have you heard someone on the golf course or at work telling you how great their stockbroker is? But how many times have you heard about the bad investments or losses they have experienced?

4. Use the Internet. As a final step before picking up the phone and calling your candidates, do some digging to discover if anyone on your list has a history of unlawful or unethical practices, or has been disciplined for any of their professional behavior or decisions. Don't worry, you don't have to hire a private investigator. You can easily find this information on the Financial Industry Regulatory Authority's (FINRA) online BrokerCheck tool: http://www.finra.org/Investors/ToolsCalculators/BrokerCheck/.

You should obviously explore the website of a potential professional and the website of the firm that they represent. The Internet allows you to go beyond the online business card of a professional to gain access to information that they don't control. It may all be good information! Or a brief search of the Internet could reveal a sketchy past. The best part is that the Internet allows you to find helpful information in an anonymous fashion.

Start with Google (www.google.com) and search the name of a potential professional and their firm. Keep your eyes trained on third party sources such as articles, blog posts or news stories that mention the professional. You can also check a professional's compliance records online with the Financial Industry Regulatory Authority (FINRA) and the Securities and Exchange Commission (SEC). If you want to dig deeper, you can combine search terms like "scams," "lawsuits," "suspensions" and "fraud" with a professional's or firm's name to see what information arises. More likely than not, you won't find anything. But if you do, you'll be glad that you checked.

HOW TO INTERVIEW CANDIDATES

After vetting your candidates and narrowing down a list of professionals that you think might be a good fit for you, it's time to start interviewing.

When you meet in person with a professional, you want to take advantage of your time with them. The presentations and information that they share with you will be important to pay attention to, but you will also want to control some aspects of the interview. After a professional has told you what they want you to hear, it's time to ask your own questions to get the specific information you need to make your decision.

Make sure to prepare a list of questions and an informal agenda so that you can keep track of what you want to ask and what points you want the professional to touch on during the interview. Using the same questions and agenda will also allow you to more easily compare the professionals after you have interviewed them all. Remember that these interviews are just that, *interviews*. You are meeting with several professionals to determine with whom you want to work. Don't agree to anything or sign anything during an interview until after you have made your final decision.

It can also be helpful to put a time limit on your interviews and to meet the professionals at their offices. The time limit will keep things on track and will allow structured time for presentations and questions/discussion. By meeting them at their office, you can get a sense of the work environment, the staff culture and attitude, and how the firm does business. If you are unable to travel to a professional's office and must meet them at your home or office, make sure that your interviews are scheduled with plenty of time between so the professionals don't cross each other's paths.

You can use the following questions during an initial interview to get an understanding of how each professional and their overall team does business and whether they are a good fit for you:

1. How do you charge for your services? How much do you charge? This information should be easy to find on their website, but if you don't see it, ask. Find out if they charge an initial planning fee, if they charge a percentage for assets under their management and if they make money by selling specific financial solutions or services. If so, you should follow up by asking how much the service costs. This will give you an idea of how they really make their money and if they have incentive to sell certain solutions over others. Make sure you understand exactly how you will be charged so there are no surprises down the road if you decide to work with this person.

2. What are the credentials, licenses, and certifications of the various team members? There are Certified Financial Planners (CFPs), Chartered Financial Consultants (ChFCs), Investment Advisor Representatives, Life Underwriter Training Council Fellows (LUTCF), Certified in Long Term Care (CLTC), Certified Public Accountants (CPAs) and Personal Financial Specialists (PFSs). Whatever their credentials or titles, you want to be sure that the professional team you work with are experts in the field relevant to your circumstances. If you want someone to manage your money, you will most likely look for an Investment Advisor. Someone that works with an independent firm will likely have a team of CPAs, CFPs and other financial experts upon whom they can draw. If you like the professional you are meeting with and you think they might be a good fit, but they don't have the accounting experience you want them to have, ask about their firm and the resources available to them. If they work closely with CPAs that are experienced in your needs, it could be a good match.

3. What are the financial services that you and your firm provide? The question within the question here is, "Can you help me achieve my goals?" Some people can only provide you with investment advice, and others are tax consultants. You will likely want to work with someone that provides a complete suite of financial planning services and solutions that touch on retirement planning, insurance options, legacy and estate structuring, and tax planning. Whatever services they provide, make sure they meet your needs and your anticipated needs.

4. What kinds of clients do you work with the most? A lot of financial professionals work within a niche: retirement planning, risk assessment, life insurance, etc. Finding someone who works with other people that are in the same financial boat as you and who have similar goals can be an important way to make sure they understand your needs. While someone might be a crackerjack annuities cowboy, you might not be interested in that option. Ask follow-up questions that will really help you understand where their expertise lies and whether or not their experience lines up with your needs.

5. May I see a sample of one of your financial plans? You wouldn't buy a car without test driving it, and you should not work with a professional without seeing a sample of how they do business. While there is no formal structure that a financial plan has to follow, the variation between professionals can help you find someone who "speaks your language." One professional may provide you with an in-depth analysis that relies heavily on info graphics and diagrams. Someone else may give you a seven page review of your assets and general recommendations. By seeing a sample plan, you can narrow down who presents information in the way that you desire and in ways that you understand.

6. How do you approach investing? You may be entirely in the dark about how to approach your investments, or you might have some guiding principles. Either way, ask each candidate what their philosophy is. Some will resonate with you and some won't. A good professional who has a realistic approach to investing won't promise you the moon or tell you that they can make you a lot of money. Professionals who are successful at retirement planning and full service financial management will tell you that they will listen to your goals, risk tolerance and comfort level with different types of investment strategies. Working with someone that you trust is critical, and this question in particular can help you find out who you can and who you can't.

7. How do you remain in contact with your clients? Does your prospective professional hold annual, quarterly or monthly meetings? How often do *you* want to meet with your professional? Some people want to check in once a year, go over everything and make sure their ducks are all in a row. If any changes over the previous year or additions to their legacy planning strategy came up, they'll do it on that date. Other people want a monthly update to be more involved in the decision making process and to understand what's happening with their portfolio. You basically need to determine the right degree of involvement for both you and your financial professional. You'll also want to feel out how your professional communicates. Do you prefer phone calls or face-to-face meetings? Do you want your professional to explain things to you in detail or to summarize for you what decisions they've made? Is the professional willing to give you their direct phone number or their email address? More importantly, do you want that information and do you want to be able to contact them in those ways?

8. Are you my main contact, or do you work with a team? This is another way of finding out how involved with you your professional will be, and how often they will meet with you. It is also a way to discover how the firm they represent operates and manages their clients. Some professionals will answer their own phone, meet with you regularly and have your home phone number on speed dial. Others will meet with you once a year and have a partner or assistant check in with you every quarter to give you an update. Other companies take an entirely team-based approach whereby clients have a main contact but their portfolio is handled by a team of professionals that represent the firm. One way isn't better than another, but one way will be best for you. Find out how the professional you are interviewing operates before entering into an agreement.

9. How do you provide a unique experience for your clients? This is a polite way of asking, "Why should I work with you?" A professional should have a compelling answer to this question that connects with you. Their answer will likely touch on their investment philosophy, their communication style and their expertise. If you hear them describing strengths and philosophies that resonate with you, keep them on your list. Some professionals will tell you that they will make investments with your money that match your values, others will say they will maximize your returns and others will say they will protect your capital while structuring your assets for income. Whatever you're looking for in a professional, you will most likely find it in the answer to this question.

This last question you will want to ask *yourself* after you've met with someone who you are considering hiring:

10. Did they ask questions and show signs that they were interested in working with me? A professional who will structure your assets to reflect your risk tolerance and to position you for a comfortable retirement must be a good listener. You will want to pass by a professional who talks non-stop and tells you what to do without listening to what you want them to do. If you felt they listened well and understood your needs, and seemed interested and experienced in your situation, then they might be right for you.

THE IMPORTANCE OF INDEPENDENCE

Not all investment firms and financial professionals are created equal. The information in this book has systematically shown that leveraging investments for income and accumulation in today's market requires new ideas and modern planning (using *new rules* versus *old rules*.) In short, you need innovative ideas to come up with the creative solutions that will provide you with the retirement that you want. Innovation thrives on independence. No matter how good a financial professional is, the firm that they represent needs to operate on principles that make sense in today's economy. Remember, advice about money has been around forever. Good advice, however, changes with the times.

Timing the market, relying on the sale of stocks for income and banking on high treasury and bond returns are not strategies. They aren't even realistic ways to make money or to generate income. Working with an independent agent can help you break free from the old ways of thinking and position you to create a realistic retirement plan.

Working with an independent professional who relies on fee-based income tied to the success of their performance will also give you greater peace of mind. When you do well, they do well, and that's the way it should be. Your independent financial professional will make sure that:

- Your assets are organized and structured to reflect your risk tolerance.
- Your assets will be available to you when you need them and in the way that you need them.
- You will have a lifetime income that will support your lifestyle through your retirement.
- You are handling your taxes as efficiently as possible.
- Your legacy is in order.
- Your Red Money is turned into Yellow Money, and is managed in your best interest.

» *Remember Marilyn and James from Chapter 1? Even though they knew they had Social Security benefits coming, they placed some money in savings and each had a pension or a 401(k).* **Before they met with a financial professional, they had no idea what their retirement would look like.** *After they met with a financial professional, they knew exactly what types of assets they had, how much they were worth, how much risk they were exposed to and how they were going to be distributed. They also created an income plan so that they could pay their bills every month the moment they retired, and they maximized their Social Security benefit by targeting the year and month they would get the most lifetime benefits. After their income needs were met, they were able to continue accumulating wealth by investing their extra assets to serve them in the future and contribute to their legacy. Their pro-*

fessional also helped them make decisions that impacted their taxes, protecting the value of their assets and allowing them to keep more of their money.

*This isn't a fairy tale scenario. This is an example of how much you stand to gain by meeting with a financial professional who can help you create a planful approach to your retirement. The concept of Know So and Hope So didn't just apply to their money, it also applied to Jack and Beverly. They **hoped** that they would have enough for retirement and that they had worked hard enough and saved enough to maintain their lifestyle. Working with a financial professional allowed them to **know** that their income needs were secured and structured to provide them with income for the rest of their lives and with some money to spare.*

Now, ask yourself: Is your retirement built on hopes and dreams, or a solid, predictable plan?

GET A SECOND OPINION... IT'S WORTH IT!

If you would get a second opinion on your health, why would you not get a second opinion on your wealth? Even if things seem fine right now, what happens when the market changes, or your life circumstances change? Are you prepared? It is much better to be proactive versus reactive.

Finding, interviewing and selecting a financial professional can seem like a daunting task. And honestly, it will take a good amount of work to narrow the field and find the one you want. In the end, it is worth the blood, sweat and tears. Your retirement, lifestyle, assets and legacy are on the line. The choices you make today will have lasting impacts on your life and the life of your loved ones. Working with someone you trust and know you can rely on to make decisions that will benefit you is invaluable. The work it takes to find them is something you will never regret.

Here is a recap of why working with a financial professional is the best retirement decision you can make:

CHAPTER 15 RECAP //

- If you feel you have more *Hope So* than *Know So* about your money and what your retirement is going to look like, working with a financial professional will give you clarity and confidence about what decisions are best for you.
- It is difficult for individual investors to not make emotional decisions about their investments. Financial professionals work with your risk tolerance, income needs and assets to find the most logical, efficient and beneficial way for you to structure your investments.
- As the DALBAR report showed, a majority of individual investors sell low when the market goes down and buy high when it goes back up. This is literally the exact opposite of what they should do to maximize their returns. Why? Emotions.
- A financial professional can help you change strategies when the market isn't going your way, but they won't abandon ship. They will stick to a planful approach. Your retirement isn't based on individual solutions or investments. It is based on a well-planned strategy that your financial professional is qualified to provide.
- Yellow Money is different from a mutual fund or a 401(k) because, while funds and 401(k)s are investment tools, they are not investment strategies. A 401(k) can be particularly misconceiving because your employer isn't truly structuring your investments inside the 401(k). They are simply providing you with a few options. The same goes for mutual funds. They are not truly managed by someone who is obligated to have your best interests and your risk tolerance in mind. In fact, the investment strategies of mutual funds change on a

regular basis, and you might not know about it until you get an annual report a *month* later.

- The biggest difference between working with a financial professional to manage your funds, and buying a mutual fund is that, while a mutual fund buys 20 stocks and pegs its earnings on the overall performance of the portfolio, a financial professional works with you to create an overall financial strategy that meets your needs. It may or may not include mutual funds.

- As an individual investor, do you really have an overarching strategy for your financial portfolio? How did you come up with your selections? Do you know how they are individually managed? Do you know how to make changes to your portfolio that reflect your risk tolerance? Do you know what your risk tolerance is?

- Managed money has a specific criteria and a professional will fit that into your overall financial plan so that it works the way you want it to.

- Not all investment firms and financial professionals are created equal. Working with an independent professional will give you more options that are customizable to your life.

- Get a second opinion.

Made in the USA
San Bernardino, CA
26 November 2014